PRAISE FOR *Room for J*

"Although not intended as a "how to" self-help book on schizophrenia, *Room for J* offers sound advice through example. For therapists, it will enlighten and inform. It will help mental health professionals to better utilize their most powerful allies: their patient's family. I intend to recommend *Room for J* to trainees and colleagues and hope that this book is widely read."

"Daniel Hanson and his family should be very proud. The entire Hanson family participated in the writing of this book, including "J" himself. The book serves as a metaphor for how persons with schizophrenia can reclaim their place in a world that too often shuns and ignores them. Through this family's experience readers will find a clear and concise roadmap to acceptance, respect, and hope."

—Xavier Amador, Ph.D. Author, *I am Not Sick, I Don't Need Help!*
Helping The Seriously Mentally Ill Accept Treatment.; Adjunct Professor,
in Clinical Psychology at Columbia University;
previously Director of Education, Research and Practice
at the National Alliance for the Mentally Ill and
Director of Psychology New York State Psychiatric Institute.

"My younger brother struggled with schizophrenia, ultimately dying at age 38. I wish Dan's book had been available for my parents and my siblings years ago. It would have affirmed all the things that we were feeling and helped us understand that we were NOT alone.

"Parents don't know what to do. They want to 'fix' their child's mental illness, to make it go away, to make it like it used to be. How do parents know what they can control and what they must accept?

Where do they find the courage to go on? This remarkable book holds out a hand to guide parents and families through the roller coaster ride of mental illness."

—Pat Koppa, President, Public Health Consultants, LLC, past Executive Director of the National Alliance for the Mentally Ill—Minnesota

"Dan Hanson poignantly captures the pain and suffering of a family as they struggle to deal with the demonic plague of schizophrenia. The honest reflections and personal journals reveal that it is not only the illness the family must battle, but also the health care and social service systems. However, the strength and the beauty of this book is that it is not a polemic railing against god and system, but rather a warm and human story of a boy and his family struggling to find a place in this world for someone who is talented and intelligent, someone who happens to see the world differently from the rest of us, and therefore marches to a different drummer. This is a must-read for any family that has been dealt the hand of schizophrenia and for others who wish to be enlightened about an illness that has the potential to affect us all as it lurks behind the curtain of consciousness."

—James Mossman, Licensed Independent Clinical Social Worker and author of *From Drying Lakes: Playing the Hand You're Dealt*

"Every publisher dreams of receiving a manuscript bearing this depth of authenticity. Daniel Hanson has integrated not only his own voice, but that of his family to tell this compelling tale of illness, hope, and a profound sense of spiritual grounding. Make room on your bookshelves and in your hearts for *Room for J*. It is the book families struggling to cope with a loved one's mental illness have long been waiting for."

—Karen Speerstra, former publisher, Butterworth Heinemann

ROOM *for* J

ROOM for J

A family struggles with schizophrenia

DANIEL S. HANSON

Beaver's Pond Press, Inc.
Edina, Minnesota

ISBN: 1-59298-082-1

Library of Congress Catalog Number: 2004113949

Book design and typesetting by Mori Studio

Printed in the United States of America

First Printing: December 2004

08 07 06 05 04   5 4 3 2 1

Beaver's Pond Press, Inc.

7104 Ohms Lane, Suite 216
Edina, MN 55439
(952) 829-8818
www.beaverspondpress.com

to order, visit www.BookHouseFulfillment.com
or call 1-800-901-3480. Reseller discounts available.

This book is dedicated to all the families
who struggle daily
to care for loved ones with schizophrenia.

TABLE
of CONTENTS

PART IV

ACKNOWLEDGEMENTS

Writing this book has been a form of therapy, a way for me to deal with my feelings by putting them on paper. It is also a way for our family to share our story so that others who struggle with schizophrenia might know that you are not alone.

Mental illness is a lonely illness. People who deal with it often feel abandoned by their family and friends. On long walks around the lake where we live, my son Joel has talked to me about how much it hurts to feel abandoned or shunned because he is labeled mentally ill. He has reminded me how important it is for people to be there for each other and to support each other.

Fortunately, we are blessed to know some very special people who refuse to abandon us even when the illness threatens to take over their lives as it has ours. Sue and I wish to acknowledge the special people in our lives. We don't know what we would have done without you.

First, we acknowledge our families. Your calls, cards and prayers were more powerful than you imagined. Just knowing that you were there for us helped Sue and me make it through the dark days. We know that J also appreciates your caring even when he says that he doesn't need it. He knows that his family still cares when others have deserted him.

Thank you to our dear friends Rick, Pam, Mike, Nita, David, Mark. You put up with our constant babbling and stuck with us when others abandoned us. Your friendship means more to us than we could ever express in words. A special "thank you" to Dorothy for being J's friend when his other friends were no longer around.

Sue and I wish to express our heartfelt gratitude to the public servants and health care professionals that have extended a helping hand when we needed it—even when it meant bucking the system. Your heroic efforts have earned our utmost respect.

My personal thanks to Louie, John, and all my friends at TCU for giving me permission to talk about things that go beyond normal business conversations. A special "thank you" to you, Louie, for reading versions of my manuscript and giving me honest, thoughtful, and caring feedback. You are indeed a true friend.

Personal thanks also go to Pat Koppa for all your great ideas and for supporting this effort. Thank you Milt and the team at Beaver's Pond Press for bringing this book to print.

There are two people we would like to acknowledge in a special way. First, James Mossman. Without you, I doubt that we would have made it through the darkest hours. We knew that you were special the first time we visited you with Joel. Our expectations were not high at the time. Our experiences with doctors and therapists up to that point had ended in disappointment. No one seemed to understand Joel. But you were different. Instead of illnesses, medications and therapies, you talked about Joel. We watched in amazement as you and Joel connected. It was as if you entered Joel's world that day. Joel followed your every word, his head nodded as if to say, "Finally someone understands me."

As I write these words of acknowledgement to you, James, I realize that you have been Joel's friend and our friend for almost ten years now. You have been with us through the good times and the bad. You have cried with us and laughed with us. You have wrestled with Joel's demons and our demons. You have stood with us in the chaos of psychiatric wards and sat with us in the peace of your quiet study. You are part of our family.

ACKNOWLEDGEMENTS

The second person we wish to acknowledge in a special way is Karen Speerstra. Karen, this is the third time you have helped me put my words on paper. You helped me share my journey through cancer when you published *A Place to Shine*. You gave voice to my struggle with corporate America with *Cultivating Common Ground*. And now you are helping us share our struggle as a family with an illness that threatens to destroy our spirit. You brought new life to this book by encouraging me to resurrect the manuscript from the shelves of my credenza. You helped shape the chapters and the words so that the true message might come out. You empowered me with your healing spirit, strengthened by your own journey through cancer, and gave me the courage to bring these words to print. For that, I will always be grateful.

INTRODUCTION

No more fiendish punishment could be devised, even were such a thing physically possible, than that one should be turned loose in society and remain absolutely unnoticed by all the members thereof.

—William James

It's been almost ten years since our son Joel declared that he was Jesus in another life and is, therefore, God. The initial shock has worn off, but we still feel the impact every day of our lives. Mental illness is like that. It doesn't go away with time. Instead it takes over lives and turns them upside down. Nothing is ever the same again.

We were hopeful at first. The doctors told us that Joel was experiencing a temporary delusional state of mind caused by a bi-polar disorder and that with medication, therapy, and time he would come to understand his illness and that his belief that he is God would go away. But time has not brought the cure that was promised. Joel's symptoms have not gone away. He still believes he is God, or a god. If anything, his belief has grown more complex and fixed in his mind.

The official diagnosis for Joel's illness has changed over the years. What was first labeled bi-polar disorder later became schizoaffective disorder or paranoid schizophrenia, depending on which doctor or therapist we choose to believe. The diagnosis is conditional. It is based on certain symptoms that change over time. Joel's symptoms include mood swings, rapid and unfocused thoughts and speech, grandiose delusions, inappropriate affect, the ability to transmit thoughts without speaking, and a growing belief that the world is against him. To those who observe Joel, these symptoms indicate that he is not in touch with reality. To Joel, on the other hand, these symptoms mean that he is connected to another more enduring and transcendent reality. Regardless of who is right, Joel, along with the rest of us, must learn to live in this reality. Joel, too, is called, as are we all, to "lieben und arbeiten (to love and to work)" as Sigmund Freud put it. And therein lies the challenge.

The medications that we were told would help Joel lead a normal life (whatever that is) have not worked as they were supposed to work. Instead of stabilizing Joel's moods and helping him accept his delusion, they have caused frightening side effects and made Joel angry at the system and those who seek to control him and take away his identity. Part of me admires Joel's feistiness while another part of me struggles to put up with his unwillingness to deal with his illness.

Unfortunately, Joel's case is not that unusual. A significant percentage of patients diagnosed with severe mental illnesses lack insight into their illness. The statistic may be as high as sixty percent according to Dr. Xavier Amador, author of *I Am Not Sick, I Don't Need Help!* We seldom hear their stories. More often we hear the success stories such as that of John Nash, the famous mathematician whose narrative was told in the popular book and movie, *A Beautiful Mind.* We forget that even Nash struggled for years before coming to grips with his illness and may never have made it were it not for the care and patience of others and the support of a protective environment.

Many people who are diagnosed with a severe mental illness struggle to live in a world that refuses to accept them. For a while their families try to care for them. But eventually their behavior wears down even those who love them. They end up in a system that recycles them from psychiatric wards to county or state hospitals to group homes to half way houses to subsidized housing, only to spiral through it all once again. This scenario goes on until they finally learn to live in society or surrender to "those who know better." We have watched worn-out and defeated victims of the system sitting in the lounges of psychiatric wards and group homes, smoking cigarettes, vacantly watching television. When they no longer find refuge in the system, some of them end up on the streets or locked tight in a prison cell. Many don't survive.

For years we tried to keep Joel out of the system. We thought we could provide a room for him at home, a safe place where he could live and be cared for until he found work and a place of his own. We helped him complete his college degree in youth and cultural studies, frequently editing Joel's papers so that his professors would understand what he was trying to say. For a while after graduating from college, Joel worked part time in various youth programs as a referee for basketball, a director of after school programs, and a childcare worker. He was wonderful with children. But it was never enough for Joel. He complained that his job was keeping him from his "godly mission." Eventually, he would stop taking his medication, leave his jobs without giving proper notice, and return to his own world of gods, aliens, and spirits, a world where anything is possible.

How naïve we were to think that we could live Joel's life for him! We assumed that because Joel was mentally ill he would accept living under the care and protection of his parents. We forgot that ill or not, Joel's spirit could not be contained within the confines of our home. Like all of us, Joel wants to make his own way. For Joel, making his own way means proving to the world that he is God and, therefore, he can do anything he sets his mind to. Our efforts to convince him to take medication that would bring him "back down to earth" are seen by Joel as attempts to control him and keep him from being who he was meant to be.

Eventually we were forced to give up on our efforts to make Joel like the rest of us. He refuses to be helped. Like so many other parents of mentally ill children, we have discovered that we cannot control Joel or cure him of his illness. All we can do is continue to love him and try to help him find a way to live in a world that, we have come to admit, has no room for him. This means we force him, against his will, to work within a system that sometimes seems to do more harm than good. Our days fill with failure. We are now submitted to Joel's belief that we are evil for even trying. All we can do is cope, one hour at a time.

Joel's mother, Sue, his brother Troy and sister Heidi and I hope and pray that Joel will gain insight into his illness or at least find a way to live in this world, even though he may never believe that he is *of* this world. We haven't given up hope, but on most days hope seems far away. On other days hope is renewed. I continue to read about longitudinal studies such as those sighted by Larry Davidson in his book *Living Outside Mental Illness.* "As many as fifty percent of patients recover from the severe effects of mental illness." However, the recovery does not happen overnight. Rather, it is a prolonged process of living for years inside the vicious cycle of mental illness and is often accompanied by debilitating side effects.

And then, of course, there is still another fifty- percent that do not make it out of the vicious cycle of mental illness. I can't help wonder which half catches Joel. As I write this, Joel was released from the hospital two days ago. He is still quite manic and psychotic. He is angry at us for not believing that he is God and for refusing to give him money to pursue a modeling career. When we fail to feed his delusions, he often threatens us with "punishment." To Joel, strongly believing he is God, punishment can range from depriving us of his company to forcing us to remain on earth. I can only imagine where that scenario places Joel. His fantasies continue to put us squarely in the dilemma: should we give him the money and feed his delusions or refuse to fund his fantasies and feel guilt and continually fear that he will harm himself?

Still, we cling to the hope that Joel will one day learn how to deal with his illness and, like Virginia Woolf, might find "a room of his own," without walking into a river with pockets full of stones.

Our friends ask us how we are able to cope. I'm never quite sure how to answer them. We live like every other couple who is forced to deal with a terrible tragedy over which they have no control. We try to do what we can to help Joel live in this world. And when we fail, we struggle to live one day at a time and hope for a miracle. And we seek to take care of ourselves as well.

I have discovered that writing helps me cope. It's cathartic. Writing helped me cope with my own throat cancer and *A Place to Shine* was the result. When I worked as a corporate executive, struggling with what seemed at times, another dysfunctional system, I wrote about releasing the power of relationships at work in a book called *Cultivating Common Ground*. And in between times, I sat at my desk at home, writing about Joel. I hoped it would help me figure him out. Later, I tried to compile what I had written into a book with a central theme and chapters that made sense. Eventually, I gave up trying. It was like trying to make sense out of Joel's illness. How can one make sense out of a terrible illness that changes someone you love into a person you hardly know and even fear at times? Most of the time, I can't even sort out my own feelings, much less his or Sue's. One day I write out of feelings of compassion while the next day all I feel is fear, frustration, and anger. But I was continually prompted to write Joel's story, not only to help our family better understand, but in the hope that others, too, could benefit.

So, what you have before you are my thoughts, as well as those of my family, including Joel. These appear in the form of "journal entries." But the bulk of the book is written through a father's perspective seeking to come to grips with the unpredictability and the unfairness of schizophrenia. Part One introduces you to Joel or J as we call him, our "Thursday's Child." In Part Two, I describe what it feels like to watch schizophrenia slowly take over our son's life. Sue and I are continually cast in the role of "Parents Without Answers." Part Three brings us up to the present, as our entire family struggles with "Living with Schizophrenia." In the final portion, Part Four, "Is There Room for J?" I try to understand what it must be like to *be* Joel, rejected and misunderstood. His own words help us understand, as do insights from other experts Sue and I have found to be of some help. It is our hope that you, too, will find partial answers here. *Partial.* Whole answers may not reside in this world. Many people who are "different" continue to struggle to find a *place,* a *room* for them. We hope our reflections are helpful for families like ours who struggle with schizophrenia. We want you to know that you are not alone. We also hope that our voices, along with the voices of others that deal with mental illness, will be heard, so that as a society we might finally make room for all our Joels.

PART I

Thursday's Child

Thursday's child has far to go.

—Anonymous

Once upon a Thursday a beautiful child was born. The youngest of three children, he had thick black hair and long black eyelashes. It all happened so fast, Dad barely had time to put on the hospital gown so that he could welcome him into the world. They named the little boy Joel after Dad's little brother who had died at birth.

The next day big Brother and Sister came to the hospital to see their new brother and were surprised at his long black hair. "He is so cute," Sister announced. "But kinda wrinkled," Brother added. They couldn't wait to take Joel home and play with him! They nicknamed him J.

J had a good childhood. As the third child, he benefited from the mistakes Mom and Dad made with the first two. If anything, he was a little spoiled. He was full of mischief, too. He loved to get Brother and Sister into trouble. Once while riding in the back seat of the car on a trip to Iowa to visit Grandma and Grandpa, J convinced Sister to put a potato chip in Brother's mouth while Brother was sleeping. "I almost choked to death," yelled Brother between coughs. The trip had been long and Mom had had enough by this time. "I love you, but you kids are driving me crazy," she shouted from the front seat. Silence followed. Finally, a small voice broke the silence. "I wub ou crazy," J said with a look of complete innocence. Mom, Dad, Brother and Sister all looked at each other at the same time. They couldn't help themselves. Everyone laughed at once.

J exhibited such self-confidence that at times he seemed arrogant. It was almost as if he had the uncanny ability to step outside himself in order to observe his own behavior, and nothing seemed to faze him. When he was just a little guy, two older boys attacked him and like any good parent, Dad jumped in to rescue J. "Pick on someone your own size!" he chastened. The bullies and Dad were surprised by J's response: "They don't bother me, they're just having fun."

J's favorite fishing spot was a big rock along the lakeshore across the street from where he lived with Mom, Dad, Brother and Sister in suburban Minneapolis. J could sit on the rock for hours casting out onto the lake. It was as if he entered a world of his own there on that rock. Everyone marveled at his patience and his skill. Grandpa said that J was a natural born fisherman because he knew where the fish were and how to lure them onto his hook without the aid of fancy fish-finders and the latest lures. It was as if he sensed it. "Fish sense" Grandpa called it. J never kept the fish he caught. Instead he gently placed them back in the water, careful not to touch their gills or to injure them in any way. Dad would watch him from a distance, awed by the graceful swing of his arm as he cast his line into the water and amazed by his seemingly endless patience.

At times, J seemed aloof or distracted from what was going on around him. He seldom showed his emotions. He never cried, not even at Grandpa's funeral, his favorite fishing buddy. Mom and Dad wondered if something was wrong, but they quickly brushed it off with the familiar line: "Every kid is different."

When J went to school, his teachers were often irritated by what they interpreted as J's aloof attitude. They saw J's lack of emotion as insolence. Mom and Dad frequently defended J, realizing that if they didn't, J's spirit would be crushed. "No one seems to understand and appreciate J," they would say to each other. But then Mom and Dad reminded themselves that J seemed to be popular and had more than enough friends.

By the time J started high school, he was a fine athlete, but he was often the first to be cut from the team. It wasn't that he lacked the talent or the skill. Indeed, he was as graceful on the basketball court as he was on the lakeshore casting for bass. But, as in fishing, J had his own way of playing basketball. To him basketball was an art form. One didn't *play* the game of basketball; rather one *became* the game of basketball. Unfortunately, J's coaches saw it differently. J's artistic perspective and his unwillingness to follow direction were perceived as having his head in the clouds or being arrogant. "He's just not coachable!"

Still, in spite of J's lack of success on the basketball court, he never stopped trying. Year after year he tried out for the team and year after year he was cut. Dad would take it hard, but J seemed to take it in stride—at least on the surface. He would tell Dad that the coaches were wrong to cut him and that he knew more about basketball than they did and that he would show them he was right. "No wonder they think he's not coachable," Dad would acknowledge to himself.

Occasionally, J's friends would take advantage of his kind nature, his aloof attitude, and his almost naïve acceptance of them. For example, there was the time they convinced J to drink straight vodka and then they dumped him off in his front yard, cold and sick. Mom and Dad were terribly upset. But J didn't seem to mind these pranks. He would never take them personally. He would tell us that he was better than his friends were and they just didn't know it yet.

ROOM *for* J

The little boy grew to be a handsome young man with the same thick black hair and long eyelashes that had wowed his family on the Thursday he was born. After high school he enrolled in a small liberal arts college. Mom and Dad had encouraged that choice because they thought the smaller class sizes and more intimate campus would be best for him. But J's trusting nature, aloof attitude, and lack of attention to details got him into trouble more than once. On one occasion his cash card was stolen. Several of his tapes and CDs were borrowed and never returned. J's efforts to make the basketball team met with the same lack of success that he experienced in high school. The other athletes made fun of him. The coach told him that he was not competitive enough. "He is too easy going," one complained. "A dreamer on the court," proclaimed another. "Too arrogant!" pronounced a third. "Not coachable," thought Dad.

In the mean time, J's dreams and visions for himself grew bigger and more grandiose. One day he announced to his family, "I've decided to become a professional basketball player so I can make lots of money. Then I'll give it to you guys so you can take care of the poor." His family tried to tell him without hurting his feelings that his chances of being a pro player were not very good, given his experiences with athletics in high school and college. But J wouldn't listen. He insisted that the coaches were all wrong and that he would prove them wrong by becoming a star like Michael Jordan. The more his family prodded J to consider another career, the more he obsessed on becoming a pro basketball star.

Mom and Dad sensed that something was far more wrong this time than the other times they had jumped in to defend J or to help him deal with reality. Unfortunately, they were right.

J's dreams and visions continued to grow bigger and bigger until one day they grew so big that they took over J's life. The little Thursday boy with the thick black hair and long eyelashes took on a mission to save the world. He talked easily of spirits, devils and aliens. He stopped eating and drinking fluids. He stayed up all night as if to defy his body. He told Mom and Dad that he must leave this world, go away with the aliens to another planet, and return some day to save the world. Mom and Dad sadly realized that life would never be the same.

The Death of a Child and the Birth of a God

There is no love in ignorance.
What I write comes from me, God, and is, therefore, the Truth.

—Joel Steven Hanson

"It's like my brother died,"
I said to my therapist.

From Troy's *Journal*

People tell us that in another time and place J could have been a shaman or a prophet. I am sure they are trying to make us feel better. But there are times when I resent their comments. What do these people know of mental illness, I ask myself. Have they lain awake all night wondering if their child will hurt himself or someone else? Do they know what it's like to live with someone who proclaims himself God and informs you in no uncertain terms that *he* has created *you?* Have they watched their child sit out in the snow for hours wearing only a light jacket, his arms stretched out to the heavens crying for the aliens to come and rescue him from a hard, cold world that doesn't recognize or appreciate him? Have they ever been forced to call the police on their own child because all of their efforts to persuade him to come in out of the cold have failed? Have they helped lock up someone they love in a psychiatric ward? Have they had their hopes dashed by a system that is not equipped to deal with the their ill child? How dare these people trivialize what we go through by simply stating "he could have been a shaman" as if conjuring up some spiritual role makes it all better?

When my anger subsides, I know that those who say this are just trying to make us feel better. I also realize that there is some truth in their words. J might have been a prophet in another time and place. He also might have been an outcast.

R. D. Laing reminds us "the cracked mind of the schizophrenic may let in light which does not enter the intact minds of many sane people whose minds are closed." Indeed, he suggests that some of the prophets in the Bible may have been schizophrenic. But he also points out that somehow each of us must learn to live in consensual reality. After living with J all these years I don't doubt for a minute that J sees and hears things that the rest of us block out. I have also come to believe that J's reality is just as legitimate as our reality and to appreciate his insights. But I know too that I must help J live in this world.

There was a time when society made room for people who lived in a different reality or as the French philosopher Michel Foucault put it, "when insanity was considered part of everyday life." But that time has long passed. Our world values only that which is reasoned and rational. Or to put it the other way, we do not value that which is not rational.

R.D. Laing also said, "If, then, he once stops pretending to be what he is not, and steps out as the person he has come to be, he emerges as Christ, or as a ghost, but not as a man; by existing with no body, he is no-body."

To exist or to be a "thing" requires a reason for existing. That which cannot be explained in rational terms is "no thing" or nothing. Therefore, someone who is mentally ill is nothing until he or she is made to be like the rest of us, rational in his or her behavior. Indeed, modern medicine is based on the premise that illness and disease can be cured, fixed, or "gotten rid of."

Joel is *not* a "no-body." He is a "some-body." But we feel him slipping away from us. We have heard other parents of mentally ill children say that it is as if their child died one piece at a time. I think about that a lot. Then I try to put myself in the place of parents I know who have lost a child. I think about my nephew who died in a terrible car accident at the tender age of two. In my mind I can still see my brother walking around in a daze as if he didn't know what to feel or where to go for consolation. I think about my friend who lost his thirteen-year-old son and how helpless I felt in the face of such profound sorrow, or my sister-in-law who lost her daughter to suicide. I marvel at the spiritual strength of my brother-in-law who lost his wife, my sister, and daughter, my niece, to cancer all within the span of two years. And I say to myself, at least Joel is still with us. But the truth is that the son we once knew is no longer with us. What's more, the life that we imagined for J will never be realized.

Like all parents we had dreams for all three of our children. But most, especially, we had dreams for Joel. Our dreams weren't specific. It was not that we expected J to be something he didn't want to be. We just wanted him to be accepted by society and to find a meaningful role that would make him feel good about himself. I suppose we assumed he would marry and have children like his brother and his sister before him. We know now that the dreams we once had for J will likely never become reality. Perhaps it is the dreams that die when someone becomes mentally ill. What we really lose when someone we love suffers from a severe mental illness is his or her potential to become a productive human being, which I suppose is why it feels like the person you love is dying. A new person emerges, someone you do not know and may even fear.

As strange as this may sound I am grateful that J believes he is God. It could be worse. He could believe that he is the devil or someone who is on a mission to purge the world of evil through whatever means are necessary. He could be Jack the Ripper or Charles Manson.

For years we would say that J may be delusional, but he is not violent. On the contrary, he is kind and gentle. He literally would not hurt a flea. Why, I've watched J save an ant from drowning in a swimming pool. I have seen him gently remove the hook from a northern pike so as not to harm the gills of the fish he just caught. I have watched the children at the daycare center where J works sit at his feet and listen to his stories. "The truth is J is about as nonviolent as one can be," I would tell people. He even refuses to watch violence on television or in the movies. He believes that all weapons of destruction should be abolished and that the police forces and armies of the world should be equipped with stun guns. J believes that he is God; his plan to change the world is grounded on his belief that love can overpower the evil forces that cause us to harm each other.

Lately, however, I have begun to question J's nonviolent nature. He has become obsessed with kickboxing. He shows his anger far more than he ever did before. On occasion he has even threatened to punish us, although his threats are usually tempered with a nonviolent form of punishment. Nonetheless, his frustration with the lack of believers in his god status and his repeated failures to live out his grandiose dreams are taking their toll on J. He grows angrier each time he fails. He believes that the world is against him, his family included. An angry and deluded young man has replaced the kind, gentle J that we once thought we knew.

J is indeed angry, and perhaps with reason, but still I believe that he would not intentionally harm others or himself. However, his belief that he is God results in behavior that threatens J's life and the lives of others. When J is psychotic he believes that he is invincible. He leaves his job at the daycare and pursues his grandiose dreams. He defies all human limits. He stops eating, drinking, and sleeping. He truly believes that he can live off his own energy. On one occasion we found J sitting in the snow with no jacket waiting to be transformed. He had been sitting there all night. Another time I rescued J from the side of a freeway. He was standing on the side of the road swaying from side to side while cars passed at seventy miles per hour. He had attempted to power his car without fuel and had run out of gas.

The challenge for us is to learn to accept J, which may require that we learn to accept J's belief that he is God and his anger with the world, including us. This does not mean that we must believe that our son *is* God or that we encourage his delusion. It simply means that we accept him, including his beliefs, even when we do not agree with him. And that we step in to save him when he defies his own limits.

It sounds so easy when I write about it, but the truth is that it's not easy at all. It's hard enough to accept that your own child believes that he is God. It's even harder to watch our son be taken over by a delusion that slowly takes him away from our world. We try to tell ourselves that it is J's illness that is responsible, but it is still hard to deal with his rejection of our efforts to love and care for him. No matter how many times we tell ourselves that it is the illness that makes J think and act the way that he does, it still hurts when he tells us that we are in the past and that he no longer needs us, or worse yet that we are evil and need to be punished by not seeing him again. It is as if our son has died and been replaced by someone we do not know and even fear at times.

We struggle to accept this terrible illness. We still love our son, but it is hard to live with God. We know that it is unlikely J will come to grips with his delusion in the near future. We have learned the hard way that trying to convince him that he is not God, through logic, is a waste of time. As our therapist puts it, "You can not reason someone out of a belief they did not reason themselves into." All that we can do is love J for who he is and hope that our son will be able to get his arms around this illness and find a way to lead a life that is worthwhile.

In some cultures people who heard voices, saw visions or lived in a transcendent reality were given a place in society and meaningful roles. Western cultures struggle to find a role for those who live in a different reality. We don't know whether to take them in or cast them out. For a while we institutionalized the mentally ill. More recently our efforts have been focused on medications that treat the symptoms. However, we continue to treat those who are ill as if they are not as "smart" as the rest of us or as worthy of our respect. We fear them and label them dangerous in spite of the evidence that shows that the number of violent crimes committed by those who are mentally ill is no larger than that of the general public.

J may not be a shaman or prophet as most of us define those roles. But J has, as prophets are wont to do, forced us to see something we would rather not confront. J has taught us to see illness as a larger healing process, not only for the person who is ill, but also for those who love and care for him. Maybe by telling J's story, he will make the world see how poorly we treat those we call mentally ill. Maybe his story will encourage us to create programs to support those who need help without disrespecting them. Maybe there will be help for us as a family. These views are what we struggle to glimpse.

Coming to Grips with a New Reality

"Dear, dear! How queer everything is today!
And yesterday things went on just as usual.
I wonder if I've been changed in the night?
Let me think: was I the same when I got up this morning?
I almost think I remember feeling a little different.
But if I'm not the same, the next question is, who in the world am I?
Ah, that's the great puzzle!"

From *Alice's Adventures in Wonderland* by Lewis Carroll

Parents live in fear of the dreaded phone call, the one with the message that their child is ill, hurt, or otherwise in trouble. The dread dissipates with time, but it never goes away completely. And then one day the phone does ring. And it *is* bad news. And what the parents dreaded so long becomes reality.

I remember our phone call as if it were yesterday. I knew it was serious when my friend pulled me out of an important meeting at work. Sue was on the phone frantically explaining that J was missing. He had called her earlier that day and left a disturbing message. In his message J said that he had run into an old friend and would call later. It wasn't the message so much as it was the sound of his voice that frightened Sue. J sounded as if he were crying. This was not at all like J. He seldom cried. He was not good at showing any emotions. It was as if he had built a wall to protect himself from being hurt. Something had to be terribly wrong for J to be crying.

We spent the next four hours searching for J. We checked all the places on campus we knew he frequented. Finally, his brother-in-law Harry found a waiter at a restaurant who recalled seeing J earlier in the day. He said he had noticed that J was different. He seemed high on life, so high that he was crying and acting strange. He was with another young man who seemed high as well. By the time our son-in-law called home with the news, J had returned.

Slowly the story unraveled. J told us that he had run into Chris, an old friend from childhood. But his friend had changed, he said. "He's now the devil, and he's looking for his other half. He's looking for me because he's looking for Christ. You see, I'm the only one who can save him, Dad. I'm his other half."

"How did you get home, J?"

"I heard Heidi calling me." J had somehow picked up his sister's voice telepathically. As he told us how the freeway traffic parted like the waters of the Red Sea to make room for him so he could get across, we noticed the pupils of his eyes were twice their normal size. His arms swung wide in animated gestures. Sue and I sat there looking at our son Joel, but seeing someone who thought he was God. We knew something was terribly wrong, but we had no idea what to do about it.

The next few days are still a blur in my mind. J continued to operate in an elated state. He would stay up all night telling us that he didn't need sleep. He talked about his ability to communicate with others telepathically, as he and Heidi had done. He announced that he had returned from a previous life when he had been Jesus and now he needed to find his friend who was his evil counterpart. In the days that followed, J roamed the city in search of his counterpart. He spent time with people on the street who he felt needed him and one night, while we were away, he brought a homeless man back with him. J's boundaries were not, we began to realize, our boundaries. J declared that he was here to save the world from evil.

In the meantime, we continued our search for help. A friend suggested that we contact a chaplain who specialized in working with young people who had experienced episodes similar to J's episode. We met with the chaplain who convinced us that what we were dealing with was even more serious than we thought it was. He told us that we needed to get J into a hospital as soon as possible before he hurt himself or someone else.

Convincing J that he needed to be in the hospital was the beginning of a long and nightmarish struggle. J didn't understand why we would think he needed help. In his manic-psychotic state he felt better than he had ever felt in his entire life, capable of "moving mountains" to use his exact words. After several hours of pleading with J, he finally agreed to go to the hospital, but only for our sakes, not his, he explained.

Sue, Heidi, and I took him to the psychiatric ward of a local hospital. After a long and frustrating struggle to convince the resident on call that J was indeed ill, he was admitted into the psychiatric ward. A friendly nurse escorted us to the ward and pulled out her key chain to unlock the door. Once through the first door she unlocked a second door. All four of us felt like we had entered a prison. I wanted to grab J, turn, and run away. Instead I put my arm around my son to reassure him.

After some brief paperwork, the nurse escorted us to the room that was to be J's quarters for the night. The room was clean and newly painted. But its bare walls still looked like a prison cell. There was no television. A man lay on one of two army cots in the room with his face to the wall. The nurse introduced J to the man. He turned to look at J. "Fuck you!" he said. One look at the expressions on our faces was enough to convince the nurse to look for an alternate room. This time J's roommate greeted him with a nod that seemed at least civil, although Joel's new roommate was obviously in a deep depression.

We spent the next hour in the lounge talking with J while a man paced the hall staring at us and spouting scripture. We must have told J at least a hundred times, "It's not so bad. Everything will be okay." J seemed just fine with the whole thing. We were the ones who needed convincing and we left the hospital feeling like traitors.

I don't remember sleeping much that night. When I closed my eyes, I could see J being attacked by the man who had sworn at him or harassed by the man who paced the halls. This, as it has turned out, was only the first of many sleepless nights. The next morning Sue and I got up early and drove to the hospital.

At the hospital, J met us with a smile. He told us how he had consoled his roommate and helped him deal with his depression. He admitted that the man who spouted scripture had come into his room and attempted to crawl in bed with him, but, J said, it wasn't anything he couldn't handle. I remember wondering who was the strong one here.

We learned that J had already met briefly with a psychiatrist earlier that morning. The psychiatrist had prescribed a medication and told him that it was okay to go home. We were furious! We had struggled so hard to convince J that he needed to enter the hospital and now an "expert" convinced him that he was just fine, that he could go home as if nothing had happened. How, we wondered, could someone see our son for fifteen minutes or less, prescribe medication and send him home? Defeat dogged our steps as we walked to the car.

Guarded hope filled the days following J's first hospital stay. In spite of our misgivings, we wanted to believe that J would return to his old self. Indeed, at first it seemed as if he might. J seemed to be calmer and more relaxed. But the calm was short-lived.

We watched Joel grow more agitated every day. He was experiencing a mental storm the likes of which we hadn't seen before. He reported that people were looking through him and reading his thoughts. He kept talking about being the messiah with a mission to save the world, and most especially, his old friend Chris. He feared that Chris was the devil and that he would return to harm him. We knew that our struggle with mental illness had just begun.

As I write these words, I still feel the sense of frustration and anger that accompanied me home from the hospital after J's first episode. I felt totally helpless and abandoned. Like Alice in Wonderland I didn't know who I was or what world I lived in. Fortunately, J's illness kept him from absorbing the magnitude of what had happened to him. But for Sue and me, a sense of the magnitude of the illness and its impact on our lives began to set in and with it, feelings of being overwhelmed. Our lives had changed. Nothing would ever be the same again. We had entered a new reality and we needed to come to grips with it, like it or not.

Part of dealing with mental illness is coming to grips with the fact that people do not look at mental illness the same way as they look at other illnesses. This is true in spite of the evidence that mental illnesses are biological in origin and therefore out of the control of the person who is ill. Many people still believe that mental illness is a sign of a weak character. Most people reserve their sympathy for people who deserve it. As a survivor of a near-fatal accident and cancer, I was awarded a badge of courage. J, on the other hand, is stamped with a stigma. As a cancer survivor, I frequently hear how brave I must be. As a person who is mentally ill, J is ignored by people who don't understand him or is treated like a child by professionals who want to control him.

I suppose we are fortunate that medications have been developed to make it possible for J to function in the "real" world most of the time. But these medications do not come without serious side effects, including tremors, loss of sexual function, cognitive and affective impairment, and even death. Furthermore, the debate over the effectiveness of medication continues. In his book *Mad in America,* Robert Whitaker suggests that the neuroleptics and mood stabilizers used to treat the mentally ill not only produce serious side effects, but also contribute to many of the symptoms associated with schizophrenia. He suggests that the medications are nothing more than a drug-induced form of a lobotomy. This leaves those of us who care for someone who is mentally ill in a terrible dilemma. We are damned if we do and damned if we don't. Going off medication results in a state of manic psychosis that can result in harm to J or others. Staying on medication induces side effects and changes in J's brain functions.

Convincing J that he needs to take medication is another part of our new reality that sounds easy but is difficult, in actuality. J refuses to accept that he is ill, and therefore, believes that he does not need medication. What's more, just because J takes his medication does not mean the world accepts J. Nor does it mean that J accepts the world. J still lives in two worlds: the transcendent world, where spirits and aliens preside, and the here-and-now world we call reality. Helping J stay grounded in this world while honoring his connections to another world is an ongoing struggle for J and for those of us who love and respect him.

The debate over medications does not stop with the side effects. We are told that Joel has certain imbalances in neurotransmitters or chemical messengers in his brain. And that neurotransmitters have names such as norepinephrine, dopamine, and serotonin. Neurotransmitters control the activity between cells in the brain. J's symptoms fall into a range of symptoms that respond better to some medication than to others. However, discovering which medication works best for J is still a long process of trial and error. To make matters more complicated, there is some evidence that neurotransmitters might not be the problem at all. Some researchers suggest that mental illness might have more to do with cell damage in the brain and that the medications may cause further damage. Elio Frattaroli suggests that psychological factors play a larger role than we think, and therefore, the patient needs fewer drugs and more psychotherapy. As J's parents we are caught in the middle, not knowing which expert to believe or what is best for our son.

The problem is more personal if you are J. Imagine being told that your brain doesn't work right and that you need medication to help it function. And oh by the way, the medication may affect your moods, change your view of life, and carry side effects that can kill you. For these and other reasons that none of us understands, J fights taking his medication. To say that it is a constant battle would be a gross understatement.

A clinical description of J's illness is helpful but it does not begin to explain the problems we face. For J, one of the biggest issues is the stigma that comes with the illness. Once people know of the illness, they discount what he believes and what he has to say. J wants to share the wisdom he has gained from connecting to the transcendent world of the spirits and aliens, as did the prophets of old. He has written a manuscript entitled *Guide to the Universe*, in which he points out the error of our ways and lays out his plan to create a better world. But the world we live in is not ready to listen to J any more than the people of old were ready to listen to the prophets. This upsets J. To J, when people discount his message they discount him. Therefore, he feels discounted as a person. The only way Joel can count in this world is to accept other people's definition of who he is and learn to play the game by the rules. For J to accept this reality is to betray his calling.

For us, the struggle with mental illness is a dual struggle. On the one hand we struggle to help Joel get his arms around his illness so that he can live grounded in this world and hopefully receive the acceptance and respect that he longs for so much while still honoring his connections to the transcendent. On the other hand we struggle with our own personal feelings of sadness, anger, and an extreme sense of loss.

Helping J deal with consensual reality is not an easy task nor is it one that we accept without question. There are times when we wonder whether we are trying too hard to make things better for J. Or are we merely trying to make J like the rest of us so that our world will come back together again? Maybe we are just making things worse. Perhaps he would have been better off had we taken a harder stance and forced him to fend for himself. There are other times when we naively think that if only we could reason with J, convince him to be like the rest of us, everything would be all better. At times we want to throw our arms around J and somehow magically turn him into the sweet little boy we once thought we knew. Other times we want to pound some sense into his head, like when he refuses to accept his illness and take the medications that would help him live a better life. Sometimes we even fear J, especially when he threatens to punish us because we refuse to believe that he is God. Most of the time we don't know what to think or do or how to feel or even whether to feel at all.

I thought that I knew all about illnesses. After all, I had survived a life-threatening car accident, bleeding ulcers, our daughter's juvenile diabetes, and a bout with cancer. But I knew nothing of illness until I confronted schizophrenia. It is like no other illness I have encountered. In spite of recent breakthroughs in our understanding of the brain, we still know so little about the causes and effects of mental illness and even less about how to cure it. The medications help, but they only treat the symptoms and often only for a while. That's if you can convince the person who is ill to take the medication. The illness itself is horrible, but that's only the half of it. With other incurable diseases, there is a measure of dignity in fighting the illness even when the battle is lost. With mental illness there is little dignity. Even when the symptoms are gone the stigma remains. Live or die, it seems as if one cannot win the battle with mental illness. The best one can do is to learn how to cope.

One Day at a Time

I am on a spiritual quest that connects to the far depths of the least advanced organisms, planets, stars, nebulas, all celestial bodies, animals, people, aliens, angels and all Godly energies.

From *J's Guide to the Universe*

J found himself in the middle of another psychotic episode. We knew it was coming. He had stopped taking his medication several days ago.

I didn't blame J. I wouldn't want to take medication that alters my brain either. But the sad truth is that when J stops taking medication, the mania takes over and the voices return. This time the aliens told him that he must abandon his job at the day care center, stay up all night, stop eating, and exercise in preparation for their coming. He had been kick boxing in the garage for hours. I wondered why he was still standing. His stamina is absolutely amazing when he gets like this. We prayed that the mania would subside and that the fall would be gentle this time. But we knew from past experience that the fall would likely be hard and J would end up in a psychiatric ward.

The other day we watched a special on John Nash, the famous mathematician who dealt with schizophrenia. He finally found a way to control the voices in his head, but it took thirty years and the help of a supportive environment that gave him space and allowed him to practice his bizarre behavior. I'm not sure we can make twenty more years even if we could find a safe environment for J outside the home. The past seven have been more than we can handle. So we decided to tell J that his home is a safe place in order to keep him off the streets. We hope that he crashes gently, and somehow we all find a way to live one day at a time.

J's doctor recommended that we call the police and have J brought into the hospital. We hesitated out of fear that J would physically resist this time and bring harm to himself. Instead we tried to convince J to go to the hospital himself. The last time J was psychotic I told him that I had heard voices from the aliens telling me that he needed to be in the hospital to minister to the people there. He bought the story then, but there was no way to know if he would buy it again. Our plan was to tell him that he needed to say a proper "good by" to his psychiatrist before he left with the aliens; once he was there, the security guards could escort him to the psychiatric ward. J, of course, would think that we tricked him and sold him to the system. In a way he would be right. But we had no choice. Without medication, J would continue to starve himself of food and sleep and descend deeper and deeper into his delusion. The last time he was in this altered god-like state he became convinced that he could absorb bullets and that no harm would come to him.

Part of me wished, again, that I could take J far away from this mess and the stress of everyday life to a place where he could live his life out in peace and be the god he wants to be. But there is no such place and, even if there were such a place, J would probably not like it there, given his desire to be with people and his love for the excitement of life. If we spent all of our time caring for J, we would have no time to care for our other children and our grandchildren. Eventually we would come to resent J. And so, we decided to do what we must in order to get J into the hospital and we would continue to live our lives, one day at a time, hoping and praying that J would learn to manage his illness and maybe even get better some day.

ONE DAY AT A TIME

There is no good way to deal with mental illness. We, for a time, tried to convince J that he had an illness not unlike his sister's diabetes. We told him that it was best for him to take his medication and reduce his level of stress but we couldn't force him. Even sending him to the hospital was no guarantee that J would accept his illness and take his medication. In fact, based on our past experiences he would play along with us long enough to get out of the hospital and then return to his old ways. And we, too, would return to living life one day at a time.

By two in the morning, in a steady falling rain, J was dancing around the swimming pool with his arms reaching out to the heavens. Occasionally he called out to the aliens. Around midnight he informed us that the aliens told him to stop eating and sleeping in preparation for his transformation to another world. "The time has come," he said. We wondered how much longer we could wait before calling the police and telling them to bring an ambulance to take him to the hospital.

I tried to talk to J. "You need to come in out of the rain."

"This world doesn't understand me," J replied. "I must leave with the aliens."

"But we need you here with us, and the children at the day care center need you," I pleaded.

"No, I must leave now. But I will return in two years to save the world and to bring you and Mom with me."

At three in the morning, we finally convinced J that he should come in out of the rain. His body was shaking from being cold and wet. Sue gave him a towel and a dry shirt. J reluctantly agreed to go to the basement window to await the coming of the aliens. One hour later, he finally collapsed on the couch. We called for the ambulance.

I stood waiting for the ambulance to arrive. Questions raced through my mind: What if the police are forced to physically take him down? Even in his exhausted state J could resist. What if he is hurt in the process?

The police were the first to arrive. I felt my knees buckle. "Dear God help us," I muttered, but to whom I was not sure.

The officers were calm. It was obvious that they had done this before. Thank God for that! By this time J had gone up to his bathroom to shave. We asked the officers if it would be okay for us to talk to J first before they escorted him to the ambulance. They agreed. The officers followed close behind us as Sue and I walked to the bathroom. "We love you J, but you need to be in the hospital," we said. The officers appeared in the doorway and J's jaw dropped. "How could you do this to me?" The officer told J that he understands his anger, but that he needs to go with them to the hospital so that he can explain his feelings to his psychiatrist. J agreed to go peacefully. We should have known he would. He has never been violent before even in a manic psychotic state. I felt terrible. I now knew what it felt like to be Judas.

We followed the ambulance to the hospital where it stopped outside the emergency room. The ambulance attendant escorted J to the admittance desk. They chatted like old friends. "We had a great conversation. He knows who I am," J announced. The attendant smiled in agreement.

It took three hours to go through the admittance process. J was not happy to be going back to the hospital, but he seemed to accept his fate. We were reminded once again of how quickly J adapts. His ability to rationalize what happens to him without giving up his belief that he is God continues to amaze me! We know from experience that he will complain about what was done to him for the next few weeks, but at least he was in the hospital and safe for now.

The next three weeks we spent talking to doctors, nurses and social workers about what to do to help J. This time he had gone too far. The doctors decided to serve commitment papers. As a result, J was forced to go to court. This offered a new experience for J and for us with new lessons to learn. For one thing, we learned that going to court was not fun. We also learned that having a good attorney who understands the system is critical. Fortunately for J the judge was a kindly man. He agreed to place J on "continuance with findings." Which meant that J would be on probation for six months during which time he must obey the doctor's orders regarding hospitalization and medication and follow a plan developed by his social worker with the intent to help J become more independent and responsible. We sighed in relief, but the relief didn't last long. J would be required to live in a group home for a few months. We were somewhat familiar with group homes from visiting Sue's niece who lived in one for several months. Our memory does not reassure us. We are back to second- guessing and worrying. "The struggle is never over," I thought to myself. "One day at a time."

From Dan's Journal:

Today is a good day. We helped J move into his room at the group home. J didn't like the idea of his living in a group home at first, but true to his way of dealing with life J has accepted the move. He even sounds a little excited about it. He was encouraged by his interview with the social worker. She assured him that they would allow him a considerable amount of freedom. Most important, she treated him with respect. I was reminded again of the simple truth that we all want to be treated with respect—even when we are ill. Why do so many people not get this, I wonder.

We are hopeful. But our hope is mixed with sadness and apprehension. We realize that this is a significant break for J. It is as if he is leaving home for the first time. The truth is this is the second time J has left home to start a new life. I recall the first time seven years earlier and the episodes that followed. So much has happened since then. This time is different, I tell myself. This time he will be watched and monitored to make sure that he takes his medication; he will be given meals and provided with support to reduce the stress of breaking away. Our sense of hope is guarded by a sense of reality born of experience. We know that J's struggle with mental illness will continue. And so will our struggle. But today is a good day. And good days are to be cherished.

Joel Steven Hanson at
his first birthday

Joel at 2 with 9-year-old brother
Troy and 6-year-old sister Heidi

An early family photo—J age 6

Ready for a day of fishing. J at $5\frac{1}{2}$

Growing up
School photos at age 9 and 13

J fishing at age 6
and at age 12

J and Dad at J's
high school graduation

This is Joel at 20, a few
months before his first
episode. He was very thin
from all the basketball he
was playing—trying to
become a "pro."

Joel Steven Hanson, age 22

J accepting his degree in youth and cultural studies

Dad and his boys on a fishing trip to Iowa in 2002

A family photo (1999)

J with his newborn
nephew Ian (2003)

Goin' fishin'
Dad (Grandpa),
Lucas, and J

PART II

PARENTS WITHOUT ANSWERS

*Do not now seek the answers which cannot be given you
because you would not be able to live them.
And the point is, to live everything. Live the questions now.*
—Rainer Maria Rilke, *Letters to a Young Poet*

FROM DAN'S JOURNAL:

*I used to think I knew a lot about mental illness. After all, I had
read Erving Goffman's* Asylums *and Ken Kesey's* One Flew over
the Cuckoo's Nest. *I had even taught courses about the impact of
social conditioning and symbolic interaction on one's perception of
what is considered normal and abnormal behavior. I really believed
that people were unfairly labeled as mentally ill when much of their
bizarre behavior was due to contingency factors. Yes, I thought I had
all the answers.*

*Living with J has convinced me that I do not have answers. I
have experienced mental illness up close and personal. I have seen
through tear-stained eyes what it can do to someone I love. I have*

experienced the helpless feeling of watching someone I love fall apart. I still believe that we judge the behavior of those who are mentally ill unfairly, stigmatize them, and treat them with disrespect, but I have a greater appreciation for the biological side of the illness. I am convinced that J does not have the ability to integrate his experiences into a self that is grounded in reality. He lives in his head.

I hate the medication. I hate what it does to J. I hate fighting with J to take it. I hate what fighting over medication has done to my relationship with J. But I also believe that J needs medication, ongoing therapy, and support in order to live in this world. I say this because I have watched J when he is not taking his medication. I have watched him sit out in the cold for hours without a jacket waiting for aliens while starving his body of food and water. I have watched him stand by the side of the road shaking from sheer exhaustion while cars sped by at 70 miles per hour. I have followed J as he wandered through an airport in a catatonic state, and I have grabbed J in my arms before he fell to ground from exhaustion and dehydration. I know that if I had not stepped in to help J on several occasions he might have died.

Watching someone I love deal with a mental illness has been by far the most difficult thing I have experienced in my life. I feel totally helpless most of the time. Nothing I do or say seems to make any difference. As much as I want J to get better, I know now that he might not get better and could even get worse. In spite of the new medications, there are no cures for schizophrenia. Current medications only treat the symptoms and sometimes not even that very effectively. What's worse, the medications have serious side effects and sometimes they cause the very symptoms they are designed to treat. And then there is the stigma that comes with mental illness. It's not fair that I earn a badge of courage for living with cancer while J gets a stigma for living with an illness that he did nothing to cause.

All of these things are so hard to deal with, but hardest of them all for me is the unpredictable and uncontrollable nature of the illness. There is not only no known cure for mental illness, there is also no way to predict how the person who is ill will behave under different situations. Living with someone who is mentally ill is living with constant fear that conflict will erupt and things will fall apart. And for me that is like living in hell.

I have never been good at dealing with conflict. "Too sensitive for your own good" was my Dad's way of putting it. He was right. I am too sensitive for my own good. It is a condition that has plagued me for years. I am always looking for ways to avoid difficult situations. Fortunately, I married Sue. She is good at conflict, which has been a blessing and a curse for me. The blessing is that I can pass the conflict to her and know that it will be handled. The curse is that it has taken me years to learn how to deal with conflict. The truth is I am still learning. It is ironic that I teach conflict management when I am the one who needs to learn the most.

After J's first episode I wanted so much to run away and hide or to give the problem to Sue to handle as I had so often done when terrible things happened to me. But I couldn't run this time. Nor could I pass the problem to Sue. She was experiencing her own shock. I was forced to deal with the illness whether I wanted to or not.

I recall the first time we took J to the emergency room at the hospital. I felt like the cowardly lion in the Wizard of Oz. I wanted so much to run away and to take J with me. "Perhaps I could find a place for him where he could be God if that's what he chooses to be," I thought to myself.

I have wanted to run away from this terrible illness numerous times since. But there is no running away from mental illness when it happens to someone you love. If we are not there for J no one else will be. There is also no cure for mental illness. One must learn to live with the illness, which means learning to live with uncertainty and conflict. It is part of living with someone who does not see the world the way that others do and refuses to accept our version of reality.

Being a parent to someone who is mentally ill in a society that does not do a good job of providing a place for those who are ill means assuming the role of primary caregiver. Since there is no place for J in society we are forced to provide a room for him. This also means that we are the ones who must deal with J when his behavior threatens his own safety or the safety of others, which puts us in a terrible bind. We must choose between J's safety and his freedom. On two occasions we have called an ambulance and the police to take him to the hospital because we feared for his life. We felt that we had no choice at the time, but the consequences of our actions have damaged our relationship. *Understandably, J no longer trusts us. I think he knows that we love him, but he also knows that we will call the authorities if necessary.*

It is hard for me to feel rejected by my own son. I doubt that J will ever appreciate our efforts to help him. Part of me doesn't blame him, but that doesn't make it any easier. I have decided that I will continue to be there for J even when he says he doesn't want me there, partly because I still believe that at some level he does want me there and partly because I need to be there for me. The truth is I need J as much as he needs me.

I still struggle to accept J and his illness. At times, I feel the only way I can survive is to keep my distance. Even writing these words in my journal is an act removed. How cowardly! Yet, like the lion in the Wizard of Oz, I have been forced to face my own lack of courage. Then there are times when I think I'm ready to face the "wicked witch." At least the lion could see her green face. Confronting mental illness is much harder. I'm not even sure what to confront. Perhaps confrontation is the wrong word. Maybe what I am dealing with is acceptance.

Whose Fault Is It?

There is only one question that really matters:
why do bad things happen to good people?
—Rabbi Kushner

By the time J became ill, the pendulum had swung away from psychological and social causes toward the biological and genetic causes. But that did not take away the guilt. We still spent hours wondering what we had done wrong. Did we over-indulge or under-indulge? Were we over protective or too lenient? Did we fight in front of J? Was it my major illnesses or some other childhood trauma? Even acknowledging the biological causes did not absolve the guilt. It only brought out a new set of questions. Was it the glass of wine we shared when Sue was pregnant? Or could the cause have been the strep throat Sue contracted during the first term of her pregnancy? Or was it merely the bad genes we carried? Both of us had relatives who struggled with mental illness. The truth is I had struggled with my own depression over the years.

Our therapist tried to convince us that J was fortunate to have parents like us. Many parents abandon their children to the system, he told us. Our commitment to work with J and provide a safe place for him to learn how to deal with his illness was to be admired. This line of reasoning helped for a while. However, it did not take away the ultimate guilt. We struggled with the biggest question of all. Why did we bring J into this world in the first place?

Dealing with the question of whether or not we had caused J's illness as well as the ultimate guilt of why we brought J into the world in the first place has been a difficult process. But it has only been part of the process. In addition to the normal feelings associated with a chronic illness, mental illness brings with it another source of guilt. The source of this guilt is brought out by the words of a woman writing an editorial following the shooting death by the police of a mentally ill man: "Why didn't his parents make sure that he took his medication?" The message in these words is that the parents are responsible for the child who is mentally ill and that if something bad happens, it is as much their fault as it is the person's who is ill. Unfortunately, the words express the view of a large number of people. In a society where the alternatives for those who deal with a mental illness are limited, the family often bears the full load of responsibility and with it the full load of guilt if something goes awry. It is a heavy load that can seem impossible to bear at times.

Another source of guilt for those who care for someone who is mentally ill emerges from the very struggle to help the person who is ill. We are beset with impossible decisions. Should we force J to take medication or risk another psychotic episode? Should we help J get off his medications in the hope that he can learn to manage his disorder and function in society? What treatment is best for J? For that matter, what treatment will he accept? No matter which way we go, it seems as if our decision is the wrong decision. For example, when we choose to force J to take his medication, we feel as if we are promoting the very symptoms that are used to diagnose his illness. On the other hand, when we choose to help J get off his medications we feel responsible for causing his psychosis.

This burden of the guilt born out of impossible decisions is made heavier when the treatment of choice is medication with serious side effects. We ask ourselves, are the medications altering J's brain in ways that affect physical and cognitive functions? This sense of guilt is made more acute by a growing controversy. Books such as *Mad in America* by Robert Whitaker and *Healing the Soul in the Age of the Brain* by Elio Frattaroli make the point that in our haste to cure mental illness we have over-emphasized the use of medications that can have harmful effects on the brain. They suggest that we are treating the symptoms in order to make people who are ill function in society, but at a price that is too high. Whitaker even suggests that high dosages of neuro-leptics are similar to a drug-induced lobotomy and that in some cases the drugs not only alter the brain, but also produce the very symptoms of the illness itself. Furthermore, he suggests that extreme cases of harmful behavior by the mentally ill often occur as a result of going off medication too quickly, implying that the medication actually contributed to the bizarre behavior. The message to us as parents is that by encouraging J to take his medication we have been destroying his brain and contributing to a vicious cycle wherein the drugs cause the very symptoms that result in the prescription of more medication. Yet, we know from painful experiences what happens when J is not on medication. So, with the help of his therapist and psychiatrist we strive to find a minimum level of medication and seek other methods such as cognitive therapy and caring support to help J live in reality. But the questions and the guilt do not go away.

There is yet another source of guilt that may be the most diffi-cult of all to deal with. Because we care for J, we have been put in the difficult position of making the decision to call an ambulance with a police escort to take him to the hospital. It is by far the most diffi-cult decision we have ever made; even when at the time it seemed justified. Intellectually, we know that had we not called, J might have died. But that didn't make the decision any easier. I can still see the police taking J to the ambulance while I stood helpless feeling like the betrayer Judas. The feeling of guilt I felt at that moment will never go away. I know that Sue feels the same.

We are learning that guilt is part of the burden of caring for someone who is mentally ill. At times we internalize the guilt and take it out on ourselves as if somehow being depressed will make it all better. At other times, we project the guilt onto something or someone else. We lash out at the system, the doctors, social workers, even J at times, although we know it is not his fault. Taking the guilt out on ourselves or on others does not make it go away. Instead, we must learn to deal with our guilt just as we must learn to deal with this awful illness that is stealing our son and our very lives out from under us.

Why Us?

I have lived on the lip
of insanity, wanting to know reasons,
knocking on a door. It opens.
I've been knocking from the inside!

—Rumi

I have never believed in fate, but every now and then I can't help asking myself the proverbial question: why us? Why do we have to go through this thing called schizophrenia? Haven't we dealt with enough illness in our family? I have tried to be rational about it. After all, we aren't the only family to deal with illness. When I look around me I know there are others who have suffered more, like my brother-in-law who lost both his wife and his daughter to cancer within two years. And what about the millions of children who suffer and die daily of starvation from poverty caused by wars, drought, and other man-made or natural disasters? Comparing our own situation to others who suffer helps for a while, but it doesn't make the question go away.

When I reflect on life, my own and others I know, I am overwhelmed with the suffering people go through and the fact that there doesn't seem to be any rhyme or reason to it. The rain falls on the good people and the bad people. The writer of the Portuguese proverb had it right. "Die young or suffer much." In fact, if I were to write another book about life, I would strongly consider titling it after the popular bumper sticker: "Shit Happens."

I sometimes wonder if life is just a series of coincidences. We try to make sense of it, but much of what we construct is post hoc rationalization. Sometimes we blame the modern madness of a mass society for the unpredictability of our lives. In desperation we long to return to a simpler, more peaceful time when life was "in harmony" with nature. But the truth is, being in harmony with nature is not what we imagine it to be. It is only an illusion we have created by distancing ourselves from the natural forces of life. Nature can be harsh at times. Just ask those who have lost loved ones to drought, floods, storms or a saber-tooth tiger.

Forces outside of our control have always threatened life. What threatens us, and therefore, what we fear the most may change, but the fear and suffering do not go away. Yesterday the threats came from natural forces; today, they come from technology. We fear airplanes crashing into buildings, viruses that might spin out of control, or bombs that can come out of nowhere. Perhaps what we fear the most are the forces we have the least control over. I find it ironic that we have given so much effort to control nature through technology only to discover that it is our technology we fear the most.

Mental illness is a reminder that in spite of our efforts to control nature and the forces around us, we cannot control them. In fact, often it seems the other way around. Illnesses enter the bodies of good people and bad people without warning or provocation. For years we tried to attribute mental illness to social causes in the hope that we could somehow get our arms around it. More recently the pendulum of blame has swung toward the biological. We scan our brains and probe our genes for the missing link. Surely if we find a cause, we reason, we will find a cure and get back into control.

No one wants to find a cause and therefore a cure for schizophrenia more than we do. Like others who deal with the unpredictable and sometimes devastating effects of mental illness, we long for a magic cure that could put our lives back in order. Our hope grows every time we hear of another breakthrough. But we know that the chances of finding a cure in our lifetime are slim. And we are left once again with the awesome challenge of finding ways to deal with the illness and the unfairness of it all, one day at a time.

In his book, *Telling Secrets*, Frederick Buechner writes about his father's suicide. He wrestles with the same proverbial question: How can a God of love allow a tragedy so horrible to take place? He never answers the question. Rather, he suggests that God does not make events happen. Instead events happen under their own steam "as random as rain." Which is to say that God is not the orchestrator of events. God does not play us like pawns in a chess game. But Buechner believes that God is present nonetheless; not as the cause, but, "as the one who even in the hardest and most hair-raising of them offers us the possibility of that new life and healing which I believe is what salvation is."

I'm not sure what I believe about God and the forces of life anymore. I do know one thing. Buechner is right. It rains in everyone's life. And sometimes when it rains, it pours. And the downpour seems to never stop. Or it stops only briefly while another cloud approaches. To us, it seemed as if J's illness was another storm in an already stormy life. At times we wonder whether the storm will ever stop.

The truth is, we are not in control of as much as we like to think we are. The bumper sticker is right. Shit *does* happen. But we can choose how we deal with the shit. We can choose to be there for each other and to care. Maybe in the end that's all any of us has: each other and a faith that somehow things will get better.

We are learning to come to grips with J's illness. We have no choice. Or I suppose we do have one choice. We could let the illness take over our lives or we can choose to find ways to live a full and meaningful life in spite of the illness—or maybe because of it. No doubt, our lives will never be the same. Some days it will feel as if we are in hell, "the valley of the shadow of death" as the Psalm reads. On these dark days all we have may be each other. Every now and then a ray of light will pierce the shadows. And we will once again get a glimpse of something out there worth believing in.

How Do You Police Your Own Child?

And yet, I'm doing it out of love, (I'm doing) things that are going to make her better. Getting her help, you know, 'cause that's the only way she's going to get better. At least that's what I tell myself.
—A retired secretary and mother
From *The Burden of Sympathy* by David Karp

FROM DAN'S JOURNAL:

Sue counted J's pills again today just to make sure he took one last night. Lately he has been skipping them. I know she'll remind him again today even though we know he hates it when we tell him what to do. We hate it too. Especially me. It's no fun policing your own adult child. Yet, I know from experience that when J goes off his medication, he stops eating and drinking and tries to find ways to leave this world.

I suppose this is not an unusual dilemma for parents who choose to care for a child who is mentally ill. But, it's especially difficult when the person who is ill refuses to accept his illness and therefore feels no need for the medication. For us, it seems to get worse as Joel's illness progresses. I remember when J was first diagnosed, it was as if a part of him realized that he was ill. Oh, sure, he balked at taking his medication, but at least he listened to our advice. Maybe it was because he was younger then, and more willing to listen to his folks. Over time, though, he has become more and more resentful of our prodding him to take his medication. Sometimes he is belligerent and even threatens to punish us.

Part of me finds it hard to blame J. I can only begin to imagine what it would be like to take orders from my parents when I was twenty-seven. Or to know that there is always the threat that they might call an ambulance to take me away and lock me up in a psychiatric ward just because I dare to declare who I believe myself to be. But sometimes I think empathizing with J only makes the problem worse.

What a dilemma! We love our son and want to be his advocate. We want to believe him when he tells us that he does not need this terrible medication that makes him feel so drowsy and causes tremors in his hands. At the same time, we fear for him. And for ourselves.

I hate forcing J to take his medication. If only there were a better way. I wish there were a place where J could go and just be who he believes himself to be—a safe place where he could be manic for awhile and preach his messages if he wants to. Maybe if we lived in a faraway tribal community things could be different. It wouldn't matter if J were a shaman, a prophet, or a clown. But I know of no village like that, certainly not here in Minnesota. I suppose we have no choice but to rely on medications and therapy to help J live in reality. It may not be the best for him or for us, but it's all we have right now. And it sure beats having him locked up in a psychiatric ward.

FROM SUE'S JOURNAL:

I'm feeling a little better right now for no apparent reason. I woke up this morning feeling completely overwhelmed by Joel's illness and, once again, at a complete loss as to how to help him. He is in the hospital again. This time we didn't do the calling. The director of the group home he had been staying in took it upon himself to make the arrangements, for which we are very grateful. Even with the knowledge that it wasn't us who actually put him there, Joel is not speaking to us or allowing us to visit. We aren't allowed through the double locked doors at the hospital. We are part of the evil forces because we agree that he needs to be there. Because J hadn't "fully decompensated" (read: "tried to harm himself"), it is going to be difficult to have him committed again, even though his commitment expired because of a county social worker's not sending in the proper paper work. The actual date for the end of the commitment isn't for another few weeks. So, I/we haven't slept well all week and in particular the past few nights.

I was near tears most of the morning. As long as I can remember, people have told me I'm a strong person, capable of handling difficult situations, good at sorting things out and finding solutions. And therein lies the problem. There seems to be very little I can do to change the situation or help Joel. For me, Mrs. Fixit, this is almost more than I can bear.

Oh, I've tried. I telephone…I call until I can't call anymore— doctors, therapists, social workers from the hospital, social workers from the county, social workers from the group home, attorneys for the county, attorneys for the hospital, medical assistance, Social Security, and the list goes on and on. Sometimes, I think I call too much. But if I don't, who will? Certainly not Joel. Because he has no insight into his illness and doesn't believe there's any problem, he prefers to throw away information from the county or the Social Security Administration. Thus, I became his authorized representative and representative payee for the above named agencies. In other words, I'm their contact regarding matters of Joel. Sometimes, I even feel that some of the calling makes a difference. For instance, Joel has been certified disabled by the Social Security Administration and the county in which we live, so he receives benefits from both. This lifted a huge financial burden from Dan and me. These agencies pay for Joel's medical costs, hospitalizations, meds, group home costs, etc. I've learned that while the paperwork is phenomenal, the staff at both of these agencies most often truly wants to help you wade your way through it all and do the best possible thing for your child.

This illness of Joel's is impossible to get your arms around. We try. We find it shapes most of our days. We're either talking about J's latest behavior or delusion and how to handle it or maybe how we didn't handle it. Or we're planning what to do to help J find a job, friends, some way to have a life.

Fortunately for me, I'm married to a man who loves to read books that really get at the nitty gritty of mental illness. I often joke that I love to read "fluff"-- mysteries, fantasy, novels, while Dan is only happy reading something that truly challenges his mind. He shares his knowledge of these authors, both current and those whose theories are still being used — R.D. Laing, Robert Whitaker, David Karp and so many others. While I've read parts of most of these books, Dan goes much deeper and thus our knowledge together is broader. We discuss the material until we both come away with a little more understanding of what J is experiencing. After nearly 40 years, Dan still amazes me.

I find I spend very little time in a nostalgic mood about what might have been. I have absolutely wonderful memories of J's childhood. Joel was our third child, a beautiful baby, loved by all four of us. Hindsight is always twenty- twenty, so when I look back now I see signs in behaviors and situations that were probably an indication of J's future problems. But at the time, his childhood and early adulthood seemed fairly normal. I repeat so often the statement, "I was a far better parent to Joel than to the other two kids." I really felt that being a little older when I had him, and already having been through parenthood twice, I was more patient with J—definitely more tolerant of most things. I can honestly say that I have very few regrets about J's childhood. I think that for the most part he was happy.

When we first learned Joel had a mental illness we both went back over and over and over what we possibly could/should have done differently. Or would it have made any difference? One day early in J's illness, we were speaking with Joel's psychiatrist and the doctor looked at Dan and me and very kindly told us J's illness was/ is biological. Period. What a blessed gift that phrase was. I suspect there's still an impact that a good or bad home life can have, but how wonderful to hear those words from a doctor.

I've learned so many things because of J's illness. I've learned that I can't always fix things and sometimes shouldn't. I've learned to love the person Joel has become even though he's nothing like what I expected. I've learned that I can live my life with a broken heart and sometimes even forget about it for awhile. And I've learned that to live in hope—hope for J's future, for new meds, for better programs for the mentally ill—is ultimately what gets me through the bad days. And I've learned to be grateful for all of it.

PART III
LIVING WITH SCHIZOPHRENIA

*As little as we know of illness, we know even less of care.
As much as the ill person's experience is denied, the caretaker's
experience is denied even more completely.*
—Arthur Frank, *At the Will of the Body*

FROM DAN'S JOURNAL:

*J stopped taking his medication last week. The symptoms of psychosis
are already showing. He is sleeping less and eating only certain foods.
He walked off his job at the day care center yesterday because he's
been communicating telepathically with an evangelist from Alabama
and has to be ready to go down there and declare himself as God. He
needs more money because he thinks he should leave tomorrow. Sue
and I fully believe that if he leaves again, we won't ever see him again.
Should we call the ambulance? Of course, the hospital won't keep him
unless it can be proven that he's a risk to himself or to others. But we
know that if not checked now, his psychosis will likely progress.*

It would be so comforting to know that J would be able to manage this time. He'll probably go off to Alabama with or without any money. I guess we'll just have to wait it out. Once again. The director at his group home agrees to watch him and keep us informed.

Sue and I were so hopeful following his last episode and commitment. The doctors and social workers had promised that this time they were going to work with J. Surely they would not drop the ball again! But it happened. Somebody forgot to file a ninety-day report and the court-ordered commitment to treatment at a group home expired. J stopped taking his medication as soon as he found out.

Things are getting worse. J called this morning to say good-bye. Sue immediately called the group home to find out from the director if J was still there. Fortunately, the director caught him packing his car and he called emergency health services. As a result, J was on his way to the hospital. Again. At least he'll be safe. For now.

A Family Affair

We are what we pretend to be,
so we must be careful about what we pretend to be.

—Kurt Vonnegut, Jr.

Mental illness is a family affair. Only one person may be diagnosed, but the illness impacts each member of the family in one way or another. We can try to run away from it, and believe me, we all have at times. But we cannot hide from it. It is there whether we want it to be or not.

J is part of our family. Therefore, he is part of our world. When one part is broken, the rest of the family doesn't work well. Our world is not the same anymore. J is part of every conversation, every holiday gathering, every evening prayer. His presence is felt whether he is at home, in the group home, in the hospital, or in Alabama.

I suspect that it is this way for most families that deal with illness. When one person is ill, we are all ill. It is a family illness, yet it is unique to each member of the family. Each of us experiences the illness in his or her own way.

FROM TROY'S JOURNAL:

"It's like my brother died," I said to my therapist. In my own battle with depression, I was spending a lot of time analyzing my feelings and relationship with my brother. When he became psychotic J had

essentially stopped existing as the person I knew and loved. But it wasn't a physical impairment or even a true chemical dependency that had robbed me of him. Those would somehow have allowed for some form of an on-going meaningful relationship in day-to-day life and conversation. It was a mental illness. Schizophrenia.

I couldn't even communicate with J any longer, even about "neutral" topics such as the weather, or sports, or girls. J, and J's world, had unique ways of interpreting the world around and outside of him. Occasionally, I could follow the thought process and, at times, even understand why someone might think the way that he did. But most of the time I simply have had to listen and feign interest in an attempt to let him know that I still care and love him enough to simply sit and listen to him ramble. Of course J had no idea that this should be difficult for anyone to do for even 5 minutes.

J and I had a unique relationship in many ways. Our seven-year age difference and a buffering sibling allowed us the opportunity to have an ideal bond. With a lack of need for competition, I could try and create and nurture the most ideal sibling friendship that I could envision. He became my playmate for sure, but in a way a surrogate son, someone I could teach and encourage to do the things that I couldn't or didn't do and watch his life unfold with pride. Except that world came crashing down for the first time at age 19 when he started to hear Michael Jordan talking directly to him through the TV and Prince writing and singing songs on the radio just for him.

When J was first hospitalized I selfishly felt like I had failed him. Here he was, out on his own using the skills to survive life that I had partially taught him. I felt like I had failed. J had left us. His super-ego had detached and created a delusional world to nurture and protect his fragile ego. And unless I was willing to enter that world, there was no place for me in it. Since then there has been little in the way of a meaningful interaction, much less a relationship. In order to relate to J in his world I must become "Buddha," the role that he has created for me. So, in many ways it is like my brother died, and unless I was willing to enter his world on his terms (and become Buddha), there was no place for me or anyone else.

It has been said that we all go through a similar grieving process in dealing with death and loss. I have been in all of the "stages"—denial, anger, rationalization—but have never been able accept his "death." Is this because I repeatedly see the person who looks and sounds like my brother, but who really no longer exists? In a way it is like seeing a living ghost who forces you to either detach or go through the grieving process every time you see him. And like most in that situation, you want to keep the ghost alive, even if it becomes a haunting. Part of you wants to keep alive the hope that his demon may be exorcised or that he will be sent back from purgatory or that he will eventually be able to come off of life-support on his own. Or what if he is kept alive with life-support measures until modern medicine finds the cure that will allow him to exist in our realm in some meaningful way? The only other alternative seems to be to give up hope and "leave him to the wolves." I am almost certain that he would be devoured. But, would that be such a terrible thing? Except, I am a doctor now and I am supposed to try and save people, or at least ease their suffering. These are the thoughts, welcome or not, that ramble through my mind.

None of the scenarios I conjure up in my mind seem probable or even possible since J is miserable when the medicines he is forced to take throw him back into our world or cause him to experience side effects. So I am left with the selfish thought that maybe J would be better off if he could leave this world, as he has often said he wants to. Of course, this would only make it easier for me to enter the acceptance stage of grieving. But accept what? That J is and will no longer be the person that he was? Everyone changes. That is part of life. Even drastic changes occur and eventually you are forced to accept these changes or come to a mutual appreciation of the differences and then move forward. But J is no longer a person. J keeps saying that he is waiting for the aliens to come and take him. Well, they already have. But they played the cruel trick of leaving the shell of J and inserting a seriously flawed replica. I have an idea for a movie title: "Schizophrenia: Invasion of the Soul Snatcher."

My only hope is that whatever is next after this life is kinder and more accepting of J. But that doesn't put my struggle to rest, because I don't necessarily believe there is anything else and J is still breathing on his own. We let people go all of the time when their body and physical brain can no longer survive on their own, while the mind and soul may very well be healthy and intact. Can't we do the same when the reverse is true? Isn't he suffering needlessly and excessively? But that is only in my eyes. I know what J thinks and that he would be happy to explain his thoughts to almost anyone willing to listen for hours, and probably without taking a breath. For that matter, we don't really know what a person who is "brain-dead" is thinking; we're left with having to interpret what they would want in that situation.

Maybe it's best to let J do what he wants to do, make some of his own mistakes and failures and see if he has any remaining ability to adapt in a meaningful way. Eventually, his delusion will "burn-out" and he will adapt. Or he won't adapt and, thus, probably not survive. In an attempt to protect itself, the delusion and illness would force him to take his own life. Kind of like an addict and their drug. The delusion allows J to escape the painful reality of day-to-day life. When reality and pain try to penetrate his world he becomes more entrenched and "addicted to his drug." Maybe the addiction is so strong because his mind, on some level, knows that it is not capable of thriving or surviving in today's world. J has always been a "health-nut" and cares a great deal about what he puts in his body. So, using drugs to escape was never really an option for J since he would never accept the toll it took on his physical health. Thus, maybe he turned to his only outlet, an emotional and mental escape. A delusion is "the ultimate high," and with some effort can be modified to counter any attack. What's more, there is no conscious insight into the disease part of the process. J not only doesn't want to change, but resists change to any extreme. Maybe an intervention and detoxification period would help. Except that we've done that before by placing him in the hospital and forcing him to take "anti-psychotic" medications.

I have so many questions and so few answers. I don't know what is right. But I do know that having a loved one with schizophrenia is very painful, a pain I feel daily, in varying degrees. I guess I will continue to try and accept J's death. I'll read other books about losing loved ones written by those who have been able to go on living and survived. I'll ponder and write in an attempt to either understand or rationalize. Hopefully, eventually, I will be able to accept.

FROM HEIDI'S JOURNAL:

Writing about J is hard for me. I'm not sure what to say or how to say it. It's like trying to describe feelings to someone. The only way that I can do it is to write J a letter.

I have known you for twenty-nine years, J. And the memories of you are many, so many that it's hard to sort them. This "disease" I guess it can be called is complex because no one knows exactly when or how it begins or whether it will ever end. I go over it in my mind trying to understand or make sense of it. Which day, which year did it get bad? After a while it all flows together and I guess all that matters is now, today. Today I know you. I watch you swim with my kids, Lucas and Danielle, at the pool and fish with Lucas down by the lake. Today you are so gentle, like a breeze.

When we were kids I would sit with you for hours. It was calming for me. You always had that in you. Even though we didn't talk the whole time, I felt close to you. We connected, a big sister with her little brother. These memories of fishing, playing tennis, video games, comfort me on some days, while other days they make me weep. I wish I had known how truly precious those times would be for me. I would have paid closer attention so that I could remember every detail later and relive it as if I was still there.

In the last few years I have become somewhat detached, distanced from you. You can be so angry, so confused, so "crazy." When I look into your eyes I don't know you. All I see is the torment of a mind that is off in another world. I want to grab you and laugh with you and look into your eyes and say, "knock it off, J. Stop kidding, it's all been a joke." But it isn't a joke. I touch you. I hug you, hoping for a reassuring squeeze. You hug back, but it feels cold. I don't want to let go. I think to myself, "Maybe if I ran away with you, I could calm you. We could live out in the country and somehow the chaos in your mind would stop." As we separate from the hug, I look directly into your eyes hoping that maybe you are there. You smile, but the warmth and the feeling I so desperately long for are missing. "Not today," I think, "I don't know you today." I will look again tomorrow. Maybe that's love, hoping that you will look at me and I will know you.

When we were kids I always thought that you and I would grow up and be friends. We would joke together like we did as kids, take family trips together, go fishing together. You and I have always been so close. I wonder how I could have spent so much time with you and not have known? You were normal, right? You were my brother.

The medications seem to make you better, but as an RN I know that they cause serious side effects and will likely hurt you. I feel as though I have betrayed our brother-to-sister oath. You looked for me to be on your side and I looked back and told you that you were crazy. I can't begin to tell you how hard it is for me to tell you that you are ill.

I have always thought that you and I were so close. We were a team. We were always going to stand up for each other. In the last eight years I don't think of us as being connected anymore. You listen to me, but we don't have a close adult relationship. The mental chaos in your head makes it hard for you to be my friend. I'm there for you, but you are not there for me. I know you love me. I know you are around, but I wonder if you are only around because every time you stop taking your medication you end up in the hospital and are "committed." I can't ask you for advice. You know very little of the things I deal with on a daily basis. You are preoccupied with your own thoughts and living in your own world. The disease takes a little more of you away each day. If you could only accept that you are ill perhaps then you could live in my reality, but you either refuse to accept or can't. And so we can't have a relationship, not here in this world anyway.

So I cherish these days with you when we can spend time together quietly, when you aren't constantly talking about your delusions and grandiose plans, which cause Lucas and Danielle to be unsure of what to do and thus avoid you. I will continue to cherish these days and try to remember every detail. I look especially deep into your eyes on days like this, for today I know you.

I guess all that is left to say is that I love you so, J. I'm so sorry I can't cure your illness and make you all better. I would do almost anything for you. I will always be there for you and hope that life holds a happy place for you somewhere, somehow.

From Lucas' Journal:

Uncle J is my friend. We go swimming together. J can stay under water for a long time. We like to go under water together and wave at each other.

I like telling J about the books I am reading. He always listens to me. Sometimes J tells me about the books that he read when he was a little boy. It's fun to talk to J. That's why I miss him so much when he is in the hospital.

My favorite thing to do with J is go fishing. J is the best fisherman I know. He always catches the most fish. I always catch fish too when I go fishing with J. He takes the fish off the hook for me so that we don't ever hurt the fish. It's so much fun to fish with J.

I wish J would never have to go to the hospital again. I know that J's brain doesn't work right sometimes, but I love him anyway.

A Frustrating Day at Court

We are still mad about the mad.
We still don't understand them and that lack of understanding
makes us mean and arrogant, and makes us mislead ourselves,
and so we hurt them.

—David Cohen

After J left his day care job to go preach in Alabama, we knew that getting him back into a program would be hard. Although he was off medication and delusional, we would still have to prove that he is at risk to harm himself or others. Because we had intervened early this time, the psychosis was not as pronounced. We knew that it was just a matter of time before J would be in trouble. He was already talking about transforming and passing on to a new realm. But the court would only look at his symptoms.

The lawyer for the hospital told us there was a new clause in the law that might help the commitment process and get J back into a program. Finally, some good news!

But elation was short-lived. We soon learned that the new clause, which is designed to commit patients like J who show a pattern of psychosis that leads to self-destructive behavior, had not been fully tested. The clause was introduced by a legislator, herself a mother of a son who struggles with mental illness. Only a few cases had come before the court.

The first day of court was another nightmare for Sue and me. By now J was in a semi-catatonic state lying in his bed at the hospital staring at the ceiling. He refused to come to court. In J's absence, his court-appointed lawyer decided to contend the constitutionality of the commitment clause, thus throwing the case into a whole new realm.

We were devastated! We realized this could go on for days while the lawyers argued over the constitutionality of a clause in the law, and in the meantime, J lay in a hospital bed staring at the ceiling waiting to transform. We turned to each other and asked, "Doesn't *anyone* care about J?"

After three hours of deliberation, the judge announced that the commitment would not be decided on the basis of the new clause and that the commitment must stand on its own merits. He called for a recess and stated that the court would re-convene in five days. The session ended. Sue left the court in tears. I followed her in a daze.

But it was a hollow victory. Five days later, we were back in court. This time the lawyer for the hospital was more confident that J would be committed. He re-framed J's case around the traditional commitment clause and plans in order to convince the judge that J should be committed on the basis that he was not able to care for himself and, consequently, presented a potential to harm himself.

Between court cases, J emerged from his catatonic state. He became extremely manic and decided to fire his lawyer and defend himself.

J entered the courtroom. He appeared confident on the outside, but on the inside his heart was pounding. The lawyers and sheriff may not have seen it, but Sue and I did. We could see his heart beating against the fabric of his shirt. It pained us to watch our son go through this demeaning process once again. Tears swelled in our eyes, and my own heart raced.

We stood as the judge entered the courtroom. J approached the judge and announced that he will defend himself. He told the judge that he was God, and therefore, more capable than anyone in the courtroom. The judge denied J's request and instructed him to sit next to his lawyer. J acquiesced only after he was told that he could take the stand in his own defense.

J's lawyer called J to the stand. For the next hour J told the court that he was God and capable of doing anything he set his mind to do. How dare we judge? He claimed nothing can harm him. We sit there fully confident that this speech will have to convince the judge to commit him. We struggle between feeling glad that he will likely be committed and receive medication and, on the other hand, feeling guilty for having helped put him in this awful place. Part of me is even proud of J. He is standing up for what he believes are his rights and freedoms. Maybe we are the ones who need help, I think to myself.

Finally, the testimony was over. J smiled, confidant that he had convinced us all of his superior being. We left the courtroom feeling sad.

Later that evening J called us from his hospital room.

"I just wanted you to know that I forgive you for what you have done to me," he says. "Wasn't I great on the stand?"

"You were great," I replied. "I was proud of you."

"I know the judge will see it my way. He knows who I am," J added.

"Yes, he knows who you are," I agreed.

J hung up the phone to meditate in his room. Sue and I cried ourselves to sleep.

Three days passed without any news from the court. We were confident that the judge would rule for a commitment, but fearful that he wouldn't and that J would again be released from the hospital. We weren't sure what we would do if that happened.

On the fourth day the attorney for the hospital called.

"I have good news," he said. "We won. The court ruled for a commitment. Now J can get help."

Sue and I told the attorney how grateful we were for his efforts. "This is best for J," we told him, but the words were hollow, as hollow as the victory in the courtroom. Inside, we felt torn apart. We had betrayed J once again. It turned out to be another sleepless night.

The Visit

"I, a stranger and afraid, in a world I never made."
—A. E. Housman

FROM DAN'S JOURNAL:

I call the operator to let me in to see J. Within a couple of minutes I hear the key enter the lock to open the door. A young woman emerges. "Who are you here to see?" "My son Joel Hanson," I reply. "Oh," she says. The staff is nice, but why is it that they always make me feel like a criminal, I wonder.

We pass through the second locked door. "Don't forget to sign in," the psych tech says in her school teacher's voice.

J's room is to the right of the front desk. He is lying on an army cot with white sheets and a flimsy blanket. The walls of his room are blank. There is no television. I would go to the bathroom, but I remember that the bathroom door is locked. I know that these precautions are necessary to prevent patients from harming themselves, but it still feels like a prison cell. A nurse peeks in and asks J how he is feeling. "Okay," he grunts. The staff is nice, but they talk to J as if he were a child. He hates that. I will never get used to the psychiatric ward, I think to myself.

J has been taking his medication for five days now. He is groggy, barely able to open his eyes. His speech is thick and muddled.

"What do you want, Dad," he asks.

"I'm just here to see you," I reply.

"Oh, I can't do anything ya know. The drugs are making me tired all the time. That's what they want, ya know. They are jealous of my power. They want me to be just like them—weaklings. It's not right to make someone do something they don't want to do."

J is obviously very angry. I don't blame him. I feel tears swelling in my eyes. I feel so bad for J. I know the medication is supposed to help him, but I wish there were another way. J is right. It's not okay to make someone do something they don't want to do. I remind myself that without medication J is harmful to himself, but it doesn't make me feel any better.

I conclude that there is nothing I can do. So I sit there and listen to J.

"They are evil. They are jealous of me. They just want to put me down. If I were out of here I could do my work. I will never be able to transform in here—too much bad energy. No one will help me."

I know that part of J's message is directed at me. Once again, my eyes brim with tears. I wish that J had the magical powers he believes that he has. Then he could fly over these walls.

But what would J do if he did get out? We'd be back to the same old pattern, I remind myself.

J is running out of words. He just wants to sleep. He tells me that I can leave. I do, but part of me stays behind.

Letting Go

Some of us, then, will leave to go live on this other planet in the Scorpio universe and the meek shall inherit the earth.

From J's Guide to the Universe

From Dan's Journal:

He has been missing for three days now. I feel helpless, my hopes dashed. I was so optimistic after he left the hospital. It seemed like J had gained some insight into his illness. I thought that maybe this time he would take his medication, return to his work at the day care, and even find a relationship. Perhaps he would find someone who would care for him as much as we do. But that was not to be. J quit taking his medication a week ago and we knew he was headed for trouble again.

Yesterday we called the police and filed a missing person report. Now all we can do is wait and hope J tries to contact us.

Sometimes I think waiting is the hardest part. I feel so helpless and hopeless; there is nothing I can do. I try sleeping, but thoughts of J clutter my mind. What if he's been involved in a car accident? What if he's on the street, or in jail? But surely someone would call if that were the case. What if he's lost his wallet or worse, what if he is unable to talk? The last time he was psychotic, he became catatonic and refused to speak to anyone.

Six p.m. and the phone rings. Thank God, it's J! But our relief is short-lived. "Dad, I'm in Newark, New Jersey. The voices told me to fly here to meet an agent who's going to help me become a famous model." Sue and I are frantic! We try to convince J to come home, but he won't listen to reason. The best we get from him is a commitment to call us in the morning.

I have been to Newark. It's not a friendly place for someone like J, but then again, where is a friendly place for J? Finally I take a sleeping pill and doze off.

When J calls back, he tells us he's decided to stay in New Jersey, "because they need me here." I remind J that he has an e-ticket and can pick it up at the airport. He refuses to listen and says he is going to contact the police to give him money. Sue, through her tears, manages to tell J that if he does that he'll wind up in prison and we won't be able to get him back to Minnesota. J agrees to take the next flight home.

Helping a child grow is to allow that child to let go. We tell each other, as parents, that this process is as natural as a robin pushing her young out of the nest, but the reality of letting go of someone we love can be very scary, indeed. Our older son, Troy, had proved throughout his adolescence that he could handle himself in spite of a few stumbles here and there. By the time Heidi was ready to leave home, we knew letting go was hard, but that things turn out okay in spite of our fears. But with J, the rules seemed to have changed.

The first time we let go of J, he returned in a manic state with a message that he was Jesus with a mission to save the world. Every effort to let go since then has resulted in a psychotic episode. I'm sure Sue and I are hanging onto J without realizing it. We are afraid to let him go because we fear he will quit taking his medication, stop eating and sleeping and wait somewhere for aliens to swoop down and take him away. Still, we wonder, are we being over-protective?

For years the psychiatric profession believed that over-protective parenting was one of the causes of mental illness. Perhaps they had things turned around. Maybe over-parenting was not the cause, but rather the result. When someone you love is ill and unable to take care of himself, the natural inclination is to step in and help.

Letting go requires trust and faith, but it is not a blind trust. When we let go, we have a vision of how things will turn out, based on some evidence. Our decision on when to let a child go is based on his proven ability to make wise decisions or to deal with difficulties. When clear evidence for making that decision is missing or worse, when the evidence runs counter, letting go is more difficult. We know that we must let go if J is ever to have a chance at an independent life, but we are scared to death that he will hurt himself or disappear and never return.

We had hoped that the group home where J lived for a time would provide him with a bridge to a more independent life. But it hasn't turned out that way, partly because J refuses to accept help and partly because the mental health system is not equipped to provide the necessary ingredients for independence such as meaningful work and independent housing.

We try to remain optimistic. We keep hoping he will find work and a safe place to live. All we can do is hope and be there for him when he falls. Letting go is hard!

ROOM *for* J

I wait at the airport for J's flight to arrive. All around me people come and go; they all look so normal. I sit next to a mother with her two children. They seem to be waiting for their Dad to return. I think back to when I was a frequent business traveler and Sue and the kids would come to the airport to wait for me. J was little then. He would smile when he saw me. I would bring them presents. So much has happened since then and now I sit here waiting for J.

They announce the arrival of his plane, but I can't spot him. I see the mother with her two kids eagerly scanning the passengers. "She's waiting for a loved one," I think. "And I'm waiting for a miracle."

A half-hour passes; then an hour. I call Sue. She is frantic. I don't know where to begin looking for J. Even if he had been on the plane, I could have missed him and he could be wandering around the airport or lost in the parking ramp. If I could find out where he left his car, maybe I could wait for him there. I go to the chauffeur stand and ask if there is any way to locate his car. After much coaxing, they agree to look for it. I give them his license plate number and within ten minutes they have located it.

I wait by his car. My cell phone rings. It is Sue. "Dan, J just called to tell us that he missed his flight and has decided to fly to California to meet with Prince and become a rock star. He wanted me to put money in his account so he could buy his ticket. What are we going to do, Dan? He's getting more delusional!" Sue explains that she begged Joel to catch the next flight home and then he can meet me at the airport so we can talk about the money he needs. J said he'd think about it.

I decide to go to my office since the next flight won't arrive for four more hours.

Back at the airport, again, I begin wondering if the security guards recognize me and take me for a terrorist checking out the terminal layout. I think I see suspicion in their eyes.

The monitor blinks to let me know the New Jersey flight is at the gate. I cross my fingers. Fifteen minutes pass. A half-hour, and still no J. Earlier I left a message on the window of his car telling him that I was waiting by the baggage claim, just in case I missed him. I call Sue to see if she knows anything. Nothing. An hour passes. I approach the woman at the ticket counter to inquire whether or not J was on that flight. She can only tell me that he had a reservation. Desperate, I ask, perhaps too loudly, if anyone can tell me whether or not my son was on that plane. A security guard invites me to check at the airport police office.

The officer at the desk looks at me suspiciously. I tell him I'm looking for my twenty-nine year old son. I plead. "He is severely psychotic and vulnerable," I explain, and then I ask him if he has a son. Finally he tells me that he will see what he can do. I wait in his office while he goes off to check and ten minutes later he returns. "Your son was on the flight," he says, and I sigh in relief until it hits me that if this is true, J has been wandering around the airport or parking lot for nearly two hours. Frantically, I dial up Sue once more and just as *the phone rings, a figure in bright red comes down the escalator. It's J! I can't believe my eyes. "Sue, he's here. I found him! It's a miracle." I can hear Sue crying on the other end, but I am now calling to J. He walks by as if in a daze. Then he drops the shopping bags he has been holding and stares straight ahead, but keeps on walking. I pick up his bags and walk beside him. "J, it's Dad." His response is slow and deliberate. "Love power. To Arizona. I need to go to Arizona," he says. I put my arm around him. "Maybe later, J. Maybe later. But for now, we're going home."*

If the Illness Doesn't Break You, the System Might

I think that the mental health system is so wound up
in eight hundred million circles…
The circles and the hoops you have to jump through are ridiculous.

From *The Burden of Sympathy* by David Karp

As I write this, Sue is on the phone again, trying to straighten out J's social security benefits. She has been trying to reach someone for days. The message on the other end of the line repeats the familiar "If you stay on the line someone will assist you." But the someone who will assist you never answers. Finally, the operator intercepts the call. "The party you are trying to reach is not answering the phone."

"Do I need her to tell me that?" Sue's frustration shows. Yesterday it was the medical assistance office. The day before that it was social services. Playing advocate for someone who is mentally ill is a full time job.

I wonder what happens to those who do not have an advocate? I suspect they are recycled through the system. Some end up sleeping on the street or languishing in prison. The mental health care system can be a nightmare to navigate for anyone. I can't imagine what it is like for someone who does not understand how things work. At times it seems as if the complexities of the system are designed to encourage people to give up in despair.

Perhaps the system is designed to help those who really need help. For those who are really down and out, there are programs to help, at least for a while. But if, like J, the patient refuses to accept his diagnosis and attempts to survive on his own, the system can be more of a hindrance than a help. Patients like J are caught in the middle. They are too functional to fit into the system, but not functional enough to be accepted by the world.

In some ways, it would appear that the system is designed to help those who are not well enough to help themselves, which is good. But for those who might benefit from gaining new skills and a sense of independence, the system falls short. To be sure there are programs for training and support, but they are often overloaded and underfunded. They can be helpful for those who accept their illness and are willing to work at menial tasks, but for patients like J who refuse to be treated as if they are sick, the system does little to provide a sense of self respect.

The court system can be another nightmare. We have gone through the process of commitment four times now. The first time was demeaning, but it was made easier by J's willingness to accept the recommendations of the hospital. The second time was another story when J insisted that he be allowed to take the stand. That time, Sue and I sat in the courtroom for four hours and watched our son be treated like a criminal. He was led to the witness stand by an armed police officer, grilled by his attorney in the presence of three social workers, a hospital attorney, a court-appointed psychologist who slept through half of the process, and a referee judge whose facial expressions moved from boredom to anger. As he rambled on about being God, we wanted to run to the stand and rescue him, but we knew that would only make matters worse. We just sat there looking down, waiting for the nightmare to be over.

The third time J was committed he was so psychotic that he was unable to appear in court. I sat in the back of the room while the attorneys argued over whether or not J was a potential harm to himself. I listened to the expert witnesses testify that my son was very ill and that the prognosis for recovery was worse each time he went off medication. J's attorney tried to argue that J was improving, but even he didn't believe it. After two hours of deliberation, the Judge turned to me and asked me whether I thought J could take care of himself. I wanted to say "yes" so that I could take J away from this nightmare and protect him from further humiliation. But I knew the honest answer was "no." I also knew that there was no way that I could save J from his self-destructive path. The hospital was the best place for him in his catatonic state. I had to say "No," knowing I was sentencing my son to six more months of commitment under court order. "It is the best option under the circumstances," I told myself.

By the time J was committed for the fourth time, one might think we would have built some immunity to the process. But we hadn't. In fact the fourth time was probably the worst. We sat through two four-hour sessions while the attorneys argued over the constitutionality of the law and waited for almost a week after that while a judge decided whether or not our son could be given help. It didn't seem to me that anyone was concerned about J. I recall wondering whether the system was *for* us or *against* us.

I do not mean to put down the many wonderful programs for the mentally ill. And I certainly do not mean to criticize the caring people who try to help in spite of the system. But the system itself makes it hard for someone who does not think like the system. The number of programs alone is enough to confuse most people. For example, as someone who is diagnosed with schizoaffective disorder, J is eligible to receive a host of benefits including Social Security benefits, medical assistance, disability income, therapy, job placement services. However, it has taken years for us to find this out. It has taken even more time to complete the paperwork and the red tape required to actually receive benefits. Finding a real person and not a computer who is willing to answer questions has been impossible at times. Sue spends hours unraveling the maze of the system and correcting errors as they occur. She is J's advocate. He's fortunate.

I'm not sure what can be done to make the system more user friendly. My hat goes off to those who try to help in spite of the system. I know that it is hard to help someone who refuses to be helped. But something needs to be done to make it easier for those who care to do their caring work. We need more advocates for J and others who struggle to survive in a world that does not have room for them. It would be wonderful if there were places where people like J could find support without feeling as if they are being treated like children. In the meantime, families like ours will be forced to be the chief caregivers and advocates. If we don't, we know no one else will.

As a society, we fail to help those who need our help the most. Maybe it's because we are mixed up. We don't know whether to push the burden on the person who is ill or on society for refusing to help. We can't decide when to protect the rights of the individual and when to step in and protect those who cannot care for themselves or keep them from harming themselves or others. We close institutions that restrict the freedoms of those who are ill, yet we fail to provide the community support they need in order to function in society. We force parents to testify against their own children in order to satisfy a system that seems as mixed up as we are.

Parents need help, themselves, to make sense of all this. When society doesn't seem to care enough to support those who need it, it puts a heavy burden on the caregivers and the load is often more than they can handle.

Not long ago we visited with the parents of two daughters. Both young women had been diagnosed with severe mental illnesses. The oldest daughter had committed suicide at the age of twenty-two. The younger daughter was in the same ward of J's hospital. In order to cope with their loss, the parents had become involved with the National alliance for the Mentally Ill (NAMI). They facilitated family support groups for parents of mentally ill children.

We sat, sharing our stories for two hours. We cried together over the loss of their child. We talked about how terrible it feels to lock up your own child because you are afraid that he or she might hurt herself or someone else. We talked about the loneliness of mental illness and how it often feels as if no one cares. We also talked about how much it means when someone does care enough to visit your child in the hospital or when someone takes the time to listen to your own struggle as parents of someone who is chronically ill. We agreed that more people need to care.

Until we as a society decide to care enough about the mentally ill to do something about our mixed up motives and mixed up systems, families will continue to bear the burden alone. One of the reasons I decided to write this book was to increase the awareness of what I call "the burden of sympathy," so that we might all be called to care. We need to find a room in our society, not just for J, but for all the mentally ill. But, of course, a "room" by itself is not enough. The "room" must be a part of a home and a community where all the members care for each other and support each other. As we begin to redefine what "room" means, I return to something Joel wrote:

> "You only define a word as something used from the past, something everyone else has used. You do not define a word as I do... as something that exists throughout all space and time, something created new right at this moment."

PART IV

Is There Room For J?

It is desirable, then, for our societal structures to be bold
and large enough to affirm rather than to destroy. . .
We are all related.

—Jamake Highwater, *The Primal Mind*

FROM DAN'S JOURNAL:

J just came to my office, in need of money because he spent $500.00 on
a fancy outfit. He is convinced that he is destined to become a famous
model. The spirits have told him so.

Once again, I explained to J the need for budgeting. I tried a
tactic that has worked in the past to discourage him from falling for
the modeling agency trap. I told him that someone as special as he
is should not limit himself to just one thing. I reminded him that he
is so good with children. He replied, "Dad, the voices tell me that I
will become a famous model." I suggested that he open his mind to
new voices. It didn't convince him, I know, but I also know from past
experience that he heard me. We hugged before he left and I told him
that I loved him. At least I feel better.

No Room in the Inn

And she gave birth to her first-born son
and wrapped him in swaddling cloths, and laid him in a manger,
because there was no place for them in the inn.

—Luke, Chapter 2, Verse 7

J believes that he was Jesus in another life, and is therefore, God. We know that he is not, but, still we can't help but notice in some ways he does resemble the biblical Jesus. Like Jesus, J does not fit in this world. There is no room for him in any "inn" we know of. The only way for J to be accepted by our world is to become just like the rest of us, and that is something he cannot do.

In his book on the history of mental illness, the French philosopher Michel Foucault examines the history of madness in the West from 1500 to 1800—from the Middle Ages, when insanity was considered part of life, to the time when mentally ill people began to be considered a threat. When the age of reason arrived, with its emphasis on that which is rational and reasoned, anything that was not rational or unreasonable was discounted—including people. Reason and the scientific mind were seen as the greatest attributes of humankind. Therefore, people who do not possess the ability to reason by linear methods are discounted. Linear thinking values "things" that can be measured. Those who live in a nonlinear reality do not value things, but rather possibilities. In fact they may not feel connected to things at all including their own bodies, which in a rational world makes them no-thing, nothing.

Robert Whitaker traces the more recent history of mental illness beginning with the era of institutions, some of which were, surprisingly, very caring places. He documents the horrible treatment of the mentally ill by those who sought to make them like the rest of us even if it required shock treatments, drowning, or removing part of their brain, right up to our current emphasis on medication. Regardless of the method, the objective has always been the same: to make the person behave just like the rest of us. In other words, we do not want anyone disrupting our well-ordered, reasoned world.

Some who are diagnosed with severe mental illness learn to adapt to a world where they do not easily fit. They are the success stories we read about in best selling books or watch on movie screens, Hollywood style. But there are a number of people like J who are not able to accept their illness even with medication. Our world would prefer that these "uncooperatives" be kept out of the mainstream. Fueled by horror stories of people who are mentally ill committing despicable crimes, our minds conjure up the worst. We prefer that these misfits be kept away from the rest of us, out of sight and out of mind. Even the system would rather not deal with those who refuse to cooperate. Thus they are left to be recycled through a system that tries to care, but too often falls short of its goals.

For years we tried to keep J out of the system by providing a room for him in our home. J welcomed the room. Believing he was God, he felt he deserved it. We tried to treat J as an adult, but it's hard not to play the parent role when your child lives with you, and especially difficult when your adult child is someone with J's illness. Our biological instincts just kick in and our caring genes take over. Because we love him, we cannot tolerate watching him being abandoned by everyone else.

As you can tell, if you've read this far, deciding to become the primary caregivers for J was not an easy decision for us to make and has been an even harder decision to implement. We now know that providing a room in our home for J is not the answer. He needs to find a room of his own. Asking Joel to remain in our care and stay in our home assumes that he is willing to accept a childlike status, which he is not. He is a young man. Providing Joel with a room in our home also assumes that we could tolerate his bizarre behavior and the constant fight over medication.

J's other option is to become a ward of the system. For those who are severely ill and do not have family to help them this is often their only option. They may appear to become more independent as a result of the programs offered, but too often it means living in crowded facilities with a roommate who is more ill than they are, moving from place to place, being endlessly recycled from the street to the hospital into a group home and then back out on the street again. After a while many of them simply give up. We have seen those who are victims of the system lounging in group homes and hospital wards, defeat written on their faces.

J could try to make it on his own, but without medication, the chances are very good that he would become psychotic again and end up in some hospital psychiatric ward. Or worse, on the street or in a prison cell. Our most vivid nightmare is having to identify J in a morgue, a victim of his own inability to know his own limits.

Not long ago I met a woman in the hospital. Her daughter had just been admitted after her fifth attempt at suicide. The mother was obviously distraught. I didn't say anything. There was nothing I could say. I just looked at her and she looked back at me. We both knew what the other was thinking. "I don't know what to do anymore," she whispered. "All I know is that I can't stop caring because if I don't care for her, no one else will." I nodded my head. We both knew the truth of those words.

Our long-term goal is to help J find a place in this world, a way to live *in* this world even though he will never be *of* this world. The hope for J and for all who struggle with mental illness is that they will find meaningful work and supportive relationships. Many of the programs for the mentally ill are designed to do just that. But the truth is that much of the work is demeaning and the relationships patronizing. To accept this, one must accept the role of someone who is *lesser*, not capable of doing "real" work and in need of help. That is not an easy thing to do for any of us. It is even harder if, like J, you believe that you are God.

At times it seems as if the cards are stacked against us. The systems designed to help people like J often do more harm than good, especially when they force caregivers to police those for whom they care for, or when they fail to provide the support needed because of impossible case loads, bureaucratic blunders, and inconsistent care. In the end, all we can do is try our best to help J find a place where he is cared for, treated with respect, given the opportunity to find work and relationships, and hope that J does the rest.

J's World

*"Well, now that we have seen each other. . . if you'll believe in me,
I'll believe in you. Is that a bargain?"*

—Alice in Wonderland, to the Unicorn

The group home experience wasn't what we had hoped it would be. Sue and I both thought that maybe J would meet others like himself there and develop relationships and learn from programs that might improve his chances for independent living. But instead, J slept half the day and came home in the afternoon to complain. He wanted to get out as soon as possible because he said, "It's so depressing! Everybody just sits around and watches TV and smokes cigarettes." He has figured out that if he goes along with the social worker, pretends to accept her "uninformed" opinion of who he really is (God, after all) and attends a few of the scheduled programs, he will get out early. "They want me to give in and become like everyone else," is the way J put it. "They're just jealous," he says. We sensed his growing anger.

I reflect on what it must be like to be J. He lives in two worlds: the world you and I call "real" and another one in some "other" dimension populated by spirits, ghosts and gods. The "real" world doesn't appreciate J's "other" world.

"Dad, I don't understand why the world has to be so cruel and competitive." He believes with all his heart that the world would be a better place if we could stop competing and live in openness and tolerance out of love for each other. But, unlike others who may totally agree with J, our son believes he is called to change the world. Sometimes J frightens people with his visions.

From J's Guide to the Universe:

In writing a book about the greatest entity or living being, God, myself, Jesus Christ reincarnated, Ishua, Jehovah, J, Joel Steven Hanson, infinitely 99.999% of the universe, the greatest individual independent being, I put much care into writing the truth. By the truth I mean every reality that I sense from my point of view. Since I know that what I say in this book is going to stretch the beliefs of people who care at all about omniscient powers, therefore everyone, and their effects on earth, I will and would like to make this as understandable as possible. Everything I say in this book will be perfect, as life, love, and goodness are all perfect they just get constantly better. Since I am God, Jesus Christ reincarnated, all the love, life and goodness, to sum it up, that exists everywhere and anywhere, I therefore am 100% perfect. I just have to grow more perfect. The men who wrote down the Bible or the people spoken of in the Bible were not totally perfect overall when they wrote down the Bible. So today we have to get past relying on the Bible to shape and determine Christian or any religious and new age philosophical beliefs so much. People today are getting much closer to being almost totally perfect for who they are, yet still you all disappoint me so by stunting my growth at times. You do this because you are jealous of me. You claim to know me and you therefore constantly give me advice and try to tell me more than I tell myself about what I should do with my life; there-

fore, everyone's life, for your life, your love and your goodness are all part of me, for I am all the love, the life, and the goodness that exists anywhere and everywhere in the universe. I am, however, and all of you will be totally and completely loving, living and good as long as you all grow the correct way.

What I know about life philosophies, Christianity and everyday life on earth more than all other things will be brought up and left for understanding in this book. I feel, think, and know that the information I give is correct enough to withstand every challenge and competing point that is brought to it.

I write as I feel, think, and know something coming from myself and all of any type of heavenly influence of me to write what I write. I am all heavenly and all healthy physical, mental, spiritual and heartfelt energy that exists anywhere and everywhere. However, as you deep down know and will know, I am the strongest individual thing that exists independently anywhere and everywhere in all creation. I am everything that is perfect, righteous, beautiful, blissful, and blessful in all areas of the universe making up infinitely 99.999% if the entire universe. The only way you all grow to be completely godly is to give gifts to people, and other physical beings to use and hope that they do not use them to enhance evil ways and change their all-good energy into evil energy which obviously has existed and still exists. As God, also in human form, I know that no one is equal to anyone totally overall because I made you, us, that way.

Please dig deeper and spend time to understand the delicate information of the delicate topics I write about. I know that people around the earth know some of the things that I know about love, life and goodness and life, for I have given them these knowledges. I have given you the parts of myself, me, that you all are these knowledges.

I must tell you now that you all have a hard time with change and proper growth because you all would call knowledges not a word, you only define a word as something used from the past, something everyone else has used. You do not define a word as I do so much, as something that exists throughout all space and time, something created new right at this moment. Only you, in all way less significant humans, consider words to be something most humans agree upon to be a word from the past set in books called dictionaries or created by other writers. So please let freedom ring and accept my new words. I warn you I will make you accept them, otherwise, and you will feel ashamed because you had no part in deciding to use the best word ever written. Why are you all scared to create new words now and in the future? Why only rely on the past for words? The past here on earth is not that good so why do you rely on it so much and neglect and abuse the gifts of the present and the future as you do not create your own language, nor do you honor, respect and understand mine well enough. You all are so scared because you not realize well enough that fear is ultimate evil so you do not change out of your state of fear because you not know the important value of changing fear to courage. You all copy other writers so much that you never create your own words and stories.

I am on a spiritual quest that connects to the far depths of the least advanced living organisms, planets, stars, nebulas, all celestial bodies, animals, people, aliens, angels and all Godly energies and ties *them all together. In my quest for perfection, I will probably come to writing a second edition of this book during my human lifetime as Joel Steven Hanson. Hopefully.*

I know, and it has been said, that ignorance is the opposite of love; there is no love in ignorance. I believe that! If one ignores something they cannot understand it ever, for they are pushing, sometimes, good things that are necessary to better their lives away from them. I ask the readers of this book to pay attention and care about what I care deeply about. I would not write this if I did not know it was worth the care of everyone.

Finally, I believe in the practice of studying what other people in your field, therefore everyone everywhere, have written, but I also believe that as humans one gets information directly from God, me, and other heavenly beings that can call themselves individuals. Please take heed and remember that infinitely 99.999% (you make up the other .001%) of our entire infinite universe, God, me, is suppose to give and receive equally, and so you as people are to give and receive equally overall.

Please take into consideration that all of these statements I make in this book are my interpretation of the truth, therefore, they are the truth.

I know that my writing style is not what most people consider perfect English literature, but I have spent many years writing the standard English—ways that are accepted by most people to be the best. I am saying that my way of writing is superior; it is the greatest and it deserves much respect from those people whom I have respected, everyone, so much by writing in their style just to be heard by their partly closed off biased hearing souls. These souls are in the people who only look for what they call perfect grammar. It is all perfect grammar, but it is not totally all completed grammar. So as I have respected standard English ways of writing by doing and being with it for infinite years, please respect, listen to, and hear my way of writing. After all, I have heard, used and respected yours. And, you can say I respected theirs, you could call it, if you are one who writes outside of the writer's playing field that is so far provided by English critiques etc. What I write comes from me, God and is therefore the Truth.

J's words are hard to understand. That is, unless you define words as J does, "as something that exists throughout all space and time, something created new right at this moment." Perhaps what J is trying to tell us is that we must read between the lines and grasp what is being said in the moment in order to understand the true meaning of his words.

When I read between the lines, the message that emerges is that he longs to be understood and appreciated. He wants to be confirmed as a special person, a person worthy of our attention and our respect.

You might wonder why J refuses to accept his illness and take advantage of the help that is offered to him. We certainly have wondered that through the years. It seems so logical. But J does not operate with the same logic that we do. And it may not even be a choice for him. In his book *I'm Not Sick, I Don't Need Help*, Xavier Amador suggests that one of the reasons patients like J refuse to accept their illness and go along with what society says about them is not a matter of choice or a result of built up defenses. Rather, it is because they can't. The illness itself prevents the brain from processing new information about the world, others, and one's self. It is as if J's self is stuck in time. To J, he was God, is God, and always will be God. For J to deny that he is God would be to deny the only identity that he has.

Xavier Amador believes that the best way to help people like J who lack insight into their illness is to treat them with respect and to show empathy. This does not mean that we need to agree with J's deluded thinking. What it means is that we give him the same respect that we all crave and deserve. From this position of mutual respect we have an opportunity to help J understand how taking medication will enable him to live in this world even though he does not see himself as grounded in this world.

There is no easy way to help J. For example, we know from experience that J is so much better when he is able to hold a job and be with friends. The problem is J's friends have abandoned him and his medication makes it difficult for him to concentrate and keep a job. In some ways it seems as if the system goes against J by setting limits on what he can earn and still receive financial and housing assistance.

Freud was right when he replied that to be sane is to be able to love and to work. We all feel better about ourselves when we have meaningful relationships and fulfilling work. Or as my wise grandmother put it, "a busy mind is a sane mind." But the system is not well equipped to help those who are ill find relationships and work. As a society, we have made progress in providing hospital care, drug therapy, and temporary housing, even though many of these facilities are over-crowded and the waiting lists are long. We have made far less progress in providing the training and support that might enable those who are ill to find meaningful work and develop relationships in the "real" world.

But I have grown to wonder more and more if our world would not be a better place if there were fewer "normal" people and more gentle souls with J's visions of how this world could be more loving. I often think to myself, "If only more people knew what a gentle, loving spirit J is. If they knew that, they would seek him out, rather than run away from him or shun him as so many do." I grow angry, at times, with those who fail to appreciate our son. Then, I remind myself that even I, his father, could not appreciate J until I let go of some of my preconceived ideas about what is "normal."

Learning to love J for who he is and to value his spiritual connections and insights into the Universe has been a journey that his whole family continues to travel. I know my own has been difficult and slow. I am still learning.

We call people like J "mentally ill." By labeling them, we excuse ourselves from their world. More importantly, we keep them from disrupting our well ordered and "in control" world. We fear the chaos that might ensue if we allowed them "in." But I am growing to believe with each passing day that our world needs to be disrupted. Perhaps we need people like J to remind us that we are not in control regardless of how much we'd like to think we are. Perhaps we need people like J to remind us that we truly are connected to the Universe, and that we do possess the power to change the world.

I once heard a priest talk about his work with the poor. He said something I will never forget: "When Jesus reminded the disciple Judas that the poor are always with us, he was not saying this so that we should go out and save the poor, but rather that the poor might save us."

But we do not appreciate the J's of our world. Instead, people like J are perceived to be out of step with the crowd.

From J's Guide to the Universe:

Whenever we follow the crowd or whenever we go with the flow we should always follow or go with just good all-loving things. Many times today many things do as others do to fit in and be like that thing because they will not be so noticeable. Well, if you are correct in your state of being and in your actions you should stand out to a degree, and never be or do bad things simply because others or the majority of people or things are bad. It is always better to be correct and loving than it is to be anything else, like evil or wrong. It is only good, then, to be, when necessary, alone for the correct reasons rather than being with something for the wrong reasons. Many people today follow the crowds that are, or go with flows that are evil and bad. They do this because they copy what others do that is bad in order to be not persecuted in any way like Jesus, Martin Luther King Junior, Gandhi, Malcolm X, etc. were, that is wrong 100%! That is a huge powerful reason why evil still exists today even though it should not exist anywhere at all. You know that, really!

J reminds us that at some level, we all know what it is like to feel out of step. The poet A.E. Housman put it this way: "…a stranger, and afraid in a world I never made." The poor and those who are out of step keep us from losing touch with the things we do not understand, yet long for. They teach us how to live out of love, to care for each other, and to be there for one another. The priest was right. The poor and the ill are here to save us, not the other way around. In *The Rainman*, with the help of his autistic brother, Raymond is able to overcome his fear, put down his mask and get back in touch with his feelings. J, too, puts us in touch with our feelings when we are around him. He challenges our fears and connects us to spiritual dimensions, like that unicorn Alice encounters. But too often we are too blind to see.

If Not God, Then Who Am I?

We are what we imagine.
Our very existence consists in our imagination of ourselves. . .
The greatest tragedy that can befall us is to go unimagined.
—N. Scott Momaday

I ask myself, "Is J so much different from the rest of us?" Don't we all want to be treated with respect and made to feel that what we do and believe in is valued? And when we are not valued, don't we all feel like retreating to another world? When we feel threatened, do we not all tend to put others down so we might look better?

Mental illness is a lonely illness. On the surface, J appears arrogant and preoccupied with himself. But this may be just a façade. Behind the bravado lies a frightened child, afraid that someone or something will reveal the truth about him and destroy his illusion.

For whatever reasons, J does not feel grounded in what we all call *reality*. His reality does not include a concept of self with a past, present, and future supported by relationships to people and events around him. It is as if his *self* is stuck in some other way of telling time. He most likely feels, as R.D. Laing puts it, "his self as partially divorced from his body." In other words, J's very being is insecure. The ordinary events of life that we take for granted threaten his low threshold of security. If J imagines something to be real, then it *is* real. This includes his own delusions.

When J declares that he is God, I become angry. How dare he be so arrogant! But J has no choice. He truly believes he is God. It is his reality. Therefore, the key to helping J is not to change his belief but rather to help him find a way to continue living in this world he finds so foreign. This is a tall order in a world that does not have room for that which is not perceived as being rational.

But imagine for a moment what it must be like to be told again and again, directly or indirectly, that your opinion does not count. Imagine what it must be like to be told repeatedly that you must take medication against your own will. Imagine living through that.

Each one of us wants to be understood and confirmed. Experts in the study of human development and communication have been telling us for years that when we treat people as if they do not count, their sense of self is damaged. In his book *The Pragmatics of Communication*, Paul Watzlawick makes the point that the confirmation we receive from other people reaffirming we are who we think we are may be the most important finding in all of communication research. Or, as the philosopher Martin Buber put it: "It is from one person to another that the heavenly bread of self-being is passed." Why would we think that people who struggle with mental illness do not need to be fed from the same "heavenly bread?"

This may be one of the most difficult yet most important lessons we have learned from J about how to deal with mental illness. J wants to be recognized and acknowledged just as we all do. Morever, he wants to be confirmed as a valued human being. Since he is not able to deal with realities as we define them, he must create his own reality. In that reality, he has a significant role that cannot be destroyed by those who put him down. What better way to do that than to become God? Sometimes this makes perfect sense to me. A frightened little boy who struggled with how to make sense of this world and his place in it cherished his arrogance as his best defense against a world that refuses to accept and confirm him.

So far, J's efforts to live in this world have failed him. I frequently go on long walks with J and we talk about all the "regular" kinds of things fathers and sons talk about. How can he find meaningful work? How can he find someone to love and be loved by? Why are we here? J finds it easy to talk about being God and he readily shares his vision of creating a better world. I used to tune out at those times. J's bizarre dreams of being God and the Universe were more than I could handle. But that was before I learned to see beyond J's words and to begin to listen with my heart instead of my head. Then I begin to hear J telling me that he wants my respect, that he wants to be seen as significant and someone who counts in this world. That is when I hear him telling me he is tired of being treated as if he were a child.

Every now and then I look into J's eyes and I see there the little boy with the thick black hair and the long black eyelashes fishing for hours on a rock. I see a nine-year old being picked on by bullies in the park. I see a teen-ager walking home from basketball practice, head down because he was cut from the team one more time. I see my little boy wanting to become a man, but not able to do it on our terms. My heart breaks for him.

So far, J's efforts to live in this world have failed because his visions for himself are unrealistic. For a while J saw himself as a professional basketball player. Then he was going to be a kick boxer and movie star like Bruce Lee. Then he saw himself as a famous model. When his plans for being a model fell through, J announced that he was going to become a rock star and tour with the rock music icon Prince. For a time, he tried to make the world accept him as a prophet. When all else fails, J falls back on his belief that he is God.

I suppose we all hold grandiose dreams for ourselves at some time or other. Eventually we are forced to accept our limits. Those lines are not clear to J. He believes everything he can imagine is real. The scary thing for Sue and me is that J seems to be running out of grandiose schemes for living in this world. Lately he has been talking about transforming himself into another dimension. Or as he states it, "passing on." It seems to him the only thing he has left to do. Being God is J's one and only true role. He cannot give it up. If he is not God, then who is he?

If We Don't Care, Who Will?

I believe that I've had some special moments that other people
don't have. . . There's probably a better word than beauty. . . I knew
that truth was a factor in it (but there is also) a certain honesty.
It was a very unguarded emotion. . . I grew up in a household with a
lot of mixed messages and never was able to trust my own emotions.
But this one came without any (difficulty). . . To truly feel my own
capacity to love, which I had not felt before, is liberating.

—A nurse and mother
From *The Burden of Sympathy* by David A. Karp

J refuses to accept that he has an illness. Part of me admires him for that. I would hate to see him give in to the system and lose his spirit. But as J's parents this puts us in a terrible bind. Do we force J to accept his illness by casting him into the system where eventually he will give in and accept that he is ill or do we attempt to help him find a way to live in the world even though he is not of the world and hope that at some point he is able to control his symptoms?

For years we tried to be sympathetic, but it's hard to sympathize with someone who refuses to play the sympathetic role. Normally we reserve our sympathy for those who show remorse or act sick—in other words those who deserve it. However, when the person who needs sympathy is your own child it changes things.

As I noted earlier, our society is confused over what to do about mental illness. We don't know whether to place the burden of caring on the individual, the family, or society. Because we are confused we move people from program to program as if they are subjects in some scientific experiment. There is little if any continuity in their care. In many cases the only constant in their lives are their families.

Caring for someone you love can be a terrible burden. Some days we simply don't know the best ways to do that. David Cohen says, "We are still mad about the mad. We still don't understand them and that lack of understanding makes us mean and arrogant, and makes us mislead ourselves, and so we hurt them."

Caring is a burden that is hard to let go, especially when you are the only one who seems to care. It is also a burden that can bring out a sense of purpose. It brings out our full potential to be human, "to truly feel the capacity of my love" as the nurse and mother put it. In order for caring to bring purpose into your life it must not stop with the person who is in need. As we have discovered for ourselves, the burden of caring can be too much to bear unless you learn to care for yourself as well.

Caring for someone who is chronically ill changes lives—not only the life of the person who is ill, but also the lives of those who care for him or her. For us, J's illness has become the center of our lives. A day doesn't pass without an issue or a crisis around J's inability to deal with our reality. It is as if our lives are absorbed by it. And at times we wonder if we are becoming the illness. We remind ourselves of the words spoken by Rabbi Hillel:"If I am not for myself, who will be for me? If I am not for others, what am I?"

In his book *On Caring* Milton Mayerhoff writes about what it means to care for someone or something. He devotes a chapter in his book to "Caring for Myself." In that chapter Mayeroff writes "Caring for myself is a species of the genus of caring'." He goes on to make a very important point. "Some of the ideas about caring become strained and artificial when applied literally to caring for myself. For instance, 'In helping others to grow, I grow as well' becomes 'In helping *myself* (italics added) grow, I grow as well' or 'In caring for another, we help him to care for himself'." It has taken a while for the meaning of Mayeroff's words to sink in, but I think I'm starting to get it.

Caring for myself means just what it says. I need to care for myself as much as I would anyone I love. This message is especially true for those of us who care for someone with a chronic illness. Caring can put meaning in our lives, but it can also be exhausting. Caring if it does not include caring for myself can bring out feelings of being trapped, which can lead to resentment, anger, and hatred. I find that when I take care of myself I feel better and have more energy to give J. I might add to Mayeroff's point that when I help myself grow, I grow as well, which enables me to care for J so that he can care for himself.

While caring for someone we love we can fall into the trap of taking responsibility for the illness. It helps to remind myself every now and then of David Karp's four C's. I didn't cause it. I can't cure it. I can't control it. All I can do is care for myself and for J. Here are some of the ways we are learning to care for ourselves.

- ◆ IT HELPS TO SET PERSONAL BOUNDARIES:
  We have discovered that it helps to set boundaries that define personal time and space, especially if you live with the person for whom you care. For example Sue and I have set aside the time from 6:00 to 10:00 p.m. for personal activities. During this time frame we have agreed that we will not discuss J's belief about being God or other issues dealing with his illness unless it is an emergency. It is a time for each of us to engage in a hobby such as reading, sewing, or writing, or for

personal reflection, or watching television. If there is an issue that needs discussing, we agree to talk about it in the morning and often set a specific time for the discussion. We also have an agreement that before interrupting an activity one must ask for and be granted permission.

✦ IT HELPS TO ESCAPE NOW AND THEN:

Another way we have learned to take care of ourselves is to escape now and then. We call them "weekend get-a-ways." We often rent a hotel room even if it is only a few miles away and stay over night. We have discovered that just being away from the illness even if it is only for a day or two helps us feel less controlled by the illness. We come home feeling refreshed and renewed. Sometimes we plan our weekend get-a-ways but more often we do them on the spur of the moment. For some reason getting away on the spur of the moment feels more liberating. I suspect it has to do with the sense of control.

✦ IT HELPS TO MAINTAIN A HOBBY:

Maintaining a hobby helps us take care of ourselves. It forces us to focus on something other than the illness. It gives us a sense of control over a part of our lives even if it is only for a while. My hobbies include writing, reading, walking, or working on the yard. Sue prefers cooking, gardening, and reading. Finding new hobbies also helps. For example, taking a class just for the sake of learning something new can offer sense of learning and growing. Lately, I have been taking guitar lessons. I am not very good at it, but that doesn't matter. I feel like I am learning and growing, which gives more energy to care for J. It also makes me feel that I am more than J's illness.

+ **IT HELPS TO HAVE OTHERS TO CARE FOR AS WELL:**

When we make J the only one we care for we find that feelings of resentment emerge. It helps to have others to care for. Both Sue and I enjoy playing with our grandchildren. They have been a godsend! We feel younger just being with them. They force us to focus on something other than J's illness.

Another godsend for me has been my students at Augsburg College, not just because they help focus my energy, but also because they listen to my story while sharing stories of their own. They remind me again that I am not alone in my struggle. Several of my students have shared stories about mental illness in their own families. Some of them have dared to share struggles of their own. I hope that I have been able to offer insight or consolation to them now and then, just as I know they have given me that and more.

Both Sue and I have benefited from getting to know other parents of mentally ill children. For one thing we have discovered that we are not alone. Another benefit from our relationships with others in similar circumstances is the support we receive and give while caring for each other. On several occasions this support has carried us through a difficult time. I am not sure what we would have done without this support. Fortunately, support groups are readily available through NAMI.

+ **IT HELPS TO EXERCISE THE BODY AS WELL AS THE MIND:**

This is another simple lesson we have learned. We feel better when we take the time to exercise our bodies. For me it is my daily walk. It serves two purposes. First, it is an opportunity to be by myself and to reflect. For me, walking is a form of meditation. Walking also refreshes my body. I feel the blood pumping through my veins. It's as if I am cleansing my body and bringing in new energy.

Some of the parents we have met through support groups work out at a health club regularly. They tell us that they not only benefit from the exercise, but also from getting away from the house for a while. Others ride a bike or use a treadmill. Whatever works for you is the best advice here.

✦ IT HELPS TO STAY CONNECTED TO THE SPIRITUAL:

This lesson is difficult to explain, given J's belief that he is God. But the truth is, J's delusion has made us look at spirituality in new ways. He challenges tradition and forces us to re-define our relationship with God. As you might imagine, it is hard to take God to church with you. But we have discovered that J's belief, even though it is delusional, has strengthened our own connection to that which transcends our understanding. We have been forced to see God in new, even bizarre ways.

I can see why some cultures found a role as prophet or shaman for people like J. He challenges my preconceived ideas and forces me to think about things in new ways. My connection to J has been our walks and fishing together. He often talks about being God and shares his spiritual insights. He describes multiple universes that are connected and talks about the power of love. His scenarios are often bizarre on the surface, but when I let go of my preconceived ideas of what spirituality should be, they force me to probe deeper and ask bigger questions of life in new ways. I now know that God is to be found in the unusual and the bizarre.

Caring for J has also helped us to find the spiritual in the everyday. In his book *Care of the Soul*, Thomas Moore suggests that the soul is found in the kitchen where meals are made and served to people we care about. His words have taken on new meaning for us. We have discovered soul in caring for J. I have personally found soul in my writing. When I write I feel connected to J, to my family, friends, and that which transcends my understanding. I have discovered that it is less important for me to define the spiritual than it is to live it and feel it.

✦ IT HELPS TO THINK OF JOB:

Another place where I have found a message of hope is in the ancient story of Job. According to the Bible and other sources of the myth, Job is portrayed as a good man. Nonetheless, he is afflicted by every plague imaginable. He loses his material goods, his children die, and his own body is covered with sores. Job struggles to make sense of his affliction. His friends try to help, but their implication that Job's bad fortune must be a punishment for some bad behavior does little to console poor Job. It is only when they listen without judging or offering solutions that they comfort Job. Job rails at God and with good cause. He cries out for answers. But God does not give Job answers. In the end, Job is forced to accept that he does not know why bad things happened to him and probably never will.

One of the messages for me from the book of Job is that God does not punish people and that bad things happen to people with no apparent cause or reason—"as random as rain" as Frederick Buechner put it. God's love comes through nonetheless—even in the midst of suffering. Perhaps even more so then. God doesn't come as the all-powerful, all-knowing God who makes the rain come down, but rather as the all-loving God who loves us and suffers with us. That thought alone comforts me when I feel as if I am receiving my unfair share of pain and suffering.

There is another message that comes to me from Job. Job's struggle is our struggle. It is part of being human and mortal. But that does not mean I should roll over and play dead. Job comes to accept the struggle, but not without a fight. He even dares to stand up to God. In his book *The First Dissident* William Safire suggests that this might be the greatest lesson from the story of Job, that Job's God not only tolerated Job's railing against him, He welcomed it. It is not in blind acceptance, but rather in the struggle that we find hope. So that as Kahlil Gibran promises in The Prophet we can "come to bless the darkness as we have blessed the light." This is a message that J would understand—perhaps better than any of us.

+ IT HELPS TO KNOW THAT I AM NOT GOD, THAT I CAN ONLY DO SO MUCH.

It helps me to know my limits. I am not God. One God in the family is enough. I can only do so much for J. In fact, I am far more helpful to J when I stop doing things *to* or *for* him and do more *with* him. The best thing I can do for J is to accept him as he is. Psychologist Karl Rogers was right about this point. When we rush in to fix things, we often make them worse. When we accept others as they are unconditionally, they begin to grow on their own. This is a hard perspective to take when the person you care for has the potential to harm himself and others. But it is true nonetheless. It requires knowing when to interfere and when not to. But most of all it requires accepting our best efforts as good enough. We can only do so much and trust the God above god to do the rest.

+ IT HELPS TO KNOW THAT OTHERS SHARE YOUR STRUGGLE.

We have found it extremely helpful to know that others deal with the same struggles that we deal with. This is where organizations such as The National Alliance for the Mentally Ill (NAMI) are so helpful. They offer family support groups, network groups and other support. There are also organizations for families that deal specifically with schizophrenia which can be accessed through the Internet. Some of these organizations provide online chat rooms and discussion groups that can be a wonderful way to share experiences and helpful advice. Many people develop lasting relationships as a result of sharing with others who know what it is like to struggle with mental illness.

♦ ACCEPTING THE FOUR C'S:

The final tip we offer is to accept the four C's. This is a tip we have taken from David Karp, author of *The Burden of Sympathy*. Karp's advice to parents and other caregivers of the mentally ill is to remember the four C's. I didn't *cause* it. I can't *cure* it. I can't *control* it. All that I can do is learn to *cope* with it. We didn't cause J's illness and as much as we try, we cannot cure him of it. Nor can we control J, as we have learned over and over again. But we can learn to cope. Based on our experiences with J, I truly believe that when we learn to accept mental illness as we would any other illness we can learn and grow from our experiences.

I would add a fifth C to those offered by Karp: to *care*. In spite of the knowledge that we did not cause J's illness and cannot cure or control it and that at times all we can do is cope, we can still care. This does not mean that we spend our days caring for J at the sacrifice of our own lives. And it definitely does not mean that we treat him as if he were a child. It simply means that we never give up hope. We never stop caring even when all we can do is to cope.

I believe, at some level, J knows that we care even when he gets angry and rejects us. I also believe, perhaps naively, that our caring will make a difference in the long run. Even if J doesn't get better, by whatever standards apply, he will always know that we love him and we care for him.

A Message of Hope

*If we are to achieve a richer culture, rich in contrasting values,
we must recognize the whole gamut of human potentialities,
and so weave a less arbitrary social fabric, one in which
each diverse human gift will find a fitting place.*

—Margaret Mead

So where do we go from here? I wish I knew the answer to that question. As I write these words, the outlook is not good for J. Once again he is in the hospital deep into his delusion. This time J has rejected everything in his past, including us. Our overtures to reach out to him are met with a blank stare or an angry rejection. There seems to be no way to get through to him. We wonder if we have lost him forever.

I know this is beginning to sound like a broken record, but living with J has convinced me that our society does not deal well with mental illness. We live in our own delusion that science and medicine have found a cure for brain disorders or at least a way to control the symptoms just like we have for diabetes or cancer. In fact, all we have discovered are anti-psychotic and mood-stabilizing drugs that treat the symptoms of the illness—and not always that very well. As noted throughout this book, there is some evidence that the medications themselves may actually contribute to the progression of the illness.

I don't mean to downplay the medical advances in the treatment of brain disorders, although I do worry about side effects. The truth is I don't know what we would do if it weren't for medications that keep

J from starving himself or putting himself in harm's way. Furthermore, I applaud the research. Like other families that deal first hand with mental illness, we would like nothing better than to learn that there is a magic medication that would allow J to function in this world. But if the research sighted earlier is accurate, a large percentage of people like J do not respond well to current medications, which leaves parents like us struggling to find hope.

While there is ample evidence for despair, I believe that there are also reasons for hope. Larry Davidson presents one of the more hopeful outlooks I have yet found in his book *Living Outside Mental Illness.* Davidson's more optimistic view is based on studies of patients with schizophrenia who found ways to break the vicious cycle of mental illness and function even in a society that is not always tolerant of differences. The factors impacting a success included a strong spirit or sense of hope on the part of the person who is ill, caring relationships based on mutual respect, an ability to work at a meaningful job, and a sense of transcendent or spiritual connections. There is no doubt that J has a strong spirit and his spiritual connections are beyond comprehension. If we can only help him find work and others to love he can then find a place in this world.

One of the truths about brain disorders is that every patient is different. Therefore, to apply the insights of Davidson or anyone else haphazardly to J would be as gross an error as to apply J's condition to your loved one. This may sound like a simple point, but it is often misunderstood. When treating brain disorders we tend to lump people into a single category as if one size fits all. But the one-size-fits-all philosophy does not apply to those who suffer with brain disorders any more than it applies to the rest of us. If this were not true, mental illness would be easy to diagnose, which any credible doctor will tell you it is not. Treatment and support programs must be tailored to meet the needs of individuals if they are to succeed. Because J does not recognize that he has a brain disorder, he needs medication that will help him gain insight into his illness. He also needs ongoing therapy from someone who will treat him with respect. But that's not enough. J needs the ongoing support of family and community that will give him a reason to want to live in this world. In this regard, J is just like you and me. He needs a self to be, others to love, and meaningful work to do. Until we provide J with these key ingredients of life, he will continue to live in his delusion and hope will die. In order to keep the hope for J and others like him alive, we as a society must do a much better job of providing a bridge to life outside mental illness.

Here, too, there is reason for hope. There is evidence that the bridge to life outside the vicious cycle of mental illness can be provided by community-based programs. Some community-based programs consist of teams made up of a social worker, a psychiatrist, a therapist, and a trained support person who can intervene in an emergency or act on behalf of the patient if necessary. In some community-based programs the support person spends time with the patient much the same as a friend might. The support person can serve a critical role here by approaching the relationship as a friendship between equals. Often just spending time with someone, going to a movie, or taking a walk while listening helps. A key ingredient of these programs is respect. Patients like J want to be treated as individuals not as "patients" and given the respect they deserve. This is an important point that is too often overlooked.

Community-based programs provide hope for stressed-out parents who have borne the burden of sympathy far too long. Unfortunately, these programs are few in numbers and often starved for funding. Current cost-cutting trends do not bode well for community-based programs. As a society, our attitude toward the mentally ill is ambivalent if not apathetic, which leaves families like ours with the bulk of the responsibility to care for those we love. Until our attitude toward caring for those who struggle with mental illness changes, families like ours will continue to struggle alone.

We live in the hope that medical research will find a cure for mental illness. Or at least that J will learn to accept his illness and find a way to live in this world. We also hope that more community-based programs will emerge to help families like ours find support in our efforts to care for our loved ones. In the meantime, we will live in hope and keep a door open and a room ready for J.

In his book *The Anatomy of Hope*, Jerome Groopman writes about people who have discovered the healing power of hope while dealing with terminal illness. He makes the important point that hope is not the same as wishful thinking, a belief that somehow things will turn out. Hope that is not grounded in reality, including the reality of a chronic illness, is false hope. True hope is hope born out of a struggle to make things better in the face of what seems at times impossible odds. True hope finds a way.

We choose to live in hope in spite of the evidence against hope, although we define hope in a different way than we used to define it. When J was first diagnosed with mental illness we hoped that he would recover from his illness and become just like the rest of us. How naïve we were to think that we could mold someone into our likeness! Through our struggles we have learned to accept J and his beliefs and a new definition of hope has emerged. The hope that I am referring to is closer to love than it is to wishful thinking. It is a hope grounded in reality, yet lifted by a vision of a world wherein there is room for J and others like him. It is a way of looking at hope that is best described by the Biblical evangelist Paul when he writes, "Love bears all things, believes all things, hopes all things, endures all things... love never ends."

Our love for J will never end, and therefore our hope will endure.

Epilogue:
GONE FISHIN'

We went fishing today. Just the three of us: J, Lucas, and I. Lucas, our nine-year-old grandson loves J with all his heart. Lucas says "J is my best buddy." They play together often. Fishing is one of their favorite things to do.

"J's got a big one!" shouts Lucas. Lucas and I watch J gradually maneuver a large Northern Pike toward shore. He plays the fish back and forth until he is able to ease it onto shore. J guides the fish toward shore with his left hand careful not to touch its gills. Gently he pulls the hook from its mouth releasing the fish into the water. We watch it swim away. I notice a look of admiration on Lucas's face.

J gives Lucas a couple of pointers about casting. Lucas follows his advice swinging his arm in a forward motion just like J showed him. After a couple of casts, Lucas has a Northern on his own line. He maneuvers the fish back and forth. Before long the fish tires and Lucas pulls it to shore. J reaches down to release the fish.

"It was a nice one, wasn't it," Lucas says while looking straight at J. "It sure was," replies J. Lucas beams from ear to ear.

What a blessing J has been for Lucas, I think to myself. Lucas has already picked up on J's gentle ways. The other day I watched him rescue a spider that was struggling to swim its way out of the water, just as I watched J do so many times.

J has a way with children and animals. It is as if they sense something in J that we adults miss. Perhaps it is J's gentle spirit or his connection to that which is pure and innocent that they sense. Whatever it is, the children know.

On days like this J seems so "normal," at least by our standards. My hope for him is renewed. I find myself believing that J will be able to get his arms around his illness. I dare to imagine that he will find someone to love and be loved by, that his work taking care of children at the day care center will satisfy his needs. After all, he is so wonderful with the children. Maybe the psychotic episodes are behind us, I tell myself.

Part of me knows that this is wishful thinking. But that's okay. Today I give myself permission to engage in wishful thinking. It is a day of fishing with my son and grandson. It is a day that will last forever in my mind.

BIBLIOGRAPHY

Amador, X, and A. Johanson. *I Am Not Sick, I Don't Need Help! Helping the Seriously Mentally Ill Accept Treatment: A Practical Guide for Families and Therapists.* New York: Vida Press, 2000.

Buechner, Frederick. *Telling Secrets.* San Francisco: Harper, 1991.

Carroll, Lewis. *Alice's Adventures in Wonderland.* Norwalk: The Easton Press, 1977.

Carse, James. *Finite and Infinite Games: A Vision of Life as Play and Possibility.* New York: Ballantine, 1986.

Davidson, Larry. *Living Outside Mental Illness: Qualitative Studies of Recovery in Schizophrenia.* New York: New York University Press, 2003.

Foucault, Michel. *Madness and Civilization: A History of Insanity in the Age of Reason.* New York: Vintage Books, 1994.

Frank, Arthur W. *At the Will of the Body: Reflections on Illness.* New York: Mariner Books, 2002.

Frattaroli, E. *Healing the Soul in the Age of the Brain: Becoming Conscious in an Unconscious World.* New York: Viking, 2001.

Goffman, Erving. *Asylums: Essays on the Social Situation of Mental Patients and Other Inmates.* New York: Anchor Books, 1961.

Groopman, Jerome. *The Anatomy of Hope: How People Prevail in the Face of Illness.* New York: Random House, 2003.

Hanson, Daniel S. *A Place to Shine: Emerging from the Shadows at Work.* Boston: Butterworth-Heinemann, 1996.

Hanson, Daniel S. *Cultivating Common Ground: Releasing the Power of Relationships at Work.* Boston: Butterworth-Heinemann, 1997.

Highwater, Jamake. *The Primal Mind: Vision and Reality in Indian America.* New York: Meridian, 1981.

Jamison, Kay Redfield. *An Unquiet Mind: A Memoir of Moods and Madness.* New York: Alfred A. Knopf, 1995.

Karp, David A. *The Burden of Sympathy: How Families Cope with Mental Illness.* New York: Oxford Press, 2001.

Kesey, Ken. *One Flew Over the Cuckoo's Nest.* New York: Signet Books, 1963.

Kushner, Harold S. *When Bad Things Happen to Good People.* New York: Avon Books, 1983.

Laing, R. D. *The Divided Self.* New York: Penguin Books, 1969.

Mayerhoff, Milton. *On Caring.* New York: Harper, 1990.

Moore, Thomas. *Care of the Soul: A Guide for Cultivating Depth and Sacredness in Everyday Life.* New York: Harper Collins, 1992.

Nasar, Sylvia. *A Beautiful Mind: The Life of Mathematician, Genius, and Nobel Laureate John Nash.* New York: Touchstone Books, 2001.

Safire, William. *The First Dissident: The Book of Job in Today's Politics.* New York: Random House, 1992.

Torrey, E. Fuller. *Surviving Schizophrenia.* 4th ed. New York: Harper Collins, 2001.

BIBLIOGRAPHY

Watzlawick, Paul. *Pragmatics of Communication: A Study of Interactional Patterns, Pathologies, and Paradoxes.* New York: W. W. Norton, 1967.

Whitaker, Robert. *Mad in America: Bad Science, Bad Medicine, and the Enduring Mistreatment of the Mentally Ill.* Cambridge: Perseus Press, 2002.

Woolis, Rebecca. *When Someone You Love has a Mental Illness: A Handbook for Family, Friends, and Caregivers.* New York: Putnam, 1992.

DANIEL S. HANSON

Daniel S. Hanson is an experienced leader, an author, and a teacher. His experiences as an executive inside corporate America prompted him to write about creating and sustaining caring work environments that bring out the best in people and organizations. He is the author of *A Place to Shine: Emerging from the Shadows at Work* and *Cultivating Common Ground: Releasing the Power of Relationships at Work.* Dan is currently a member of the faculty at Augsburg College, where he teaches courses in Communication.

Dan and his wife Sue are also the parents of a son, Joel, who struggles with a severe mental illness. It is this experience that prompted Dan to write *Room for J.* Dan and Sue are committed to help other parents who struggle to care for someone who does not willingly accept their care. Dan and Sue live on a small lake in Maple Grove, Minnesota.

NOTES

DATE DUE		
JUL 3 0 2005		
JAN 0 9 2006		
MAR 1 6 2007		
OCT 2 6 200V		
DEC 1 9 2008		